Where Angels Fear to Tread
Finding Balance Through Breast Cancer

Where Angels Fear to Tread

Finding balance through breast cancer

KIM HENDERSON

Copyright © 2019 Kim Henderson

All rights reserved. No part of this book may be reproduced by any mechanical, photographic or electronic process, including photocopying, recording, taping, or by any information storage retrieval system—except for brief quotations embodied in articles and reviews—without written permission from the author.

The author of this book does not dispense medical advice or prescribe the use of any technique as a form of treatment for physical, emotional or medical problems without the advice of a physician, either directly or indirectly. The intent of the author is only to offer information of a general nature to help you in your quest for emotional and spiritual well-being. In the event you use any of the information in this book for yourself, the author/publisher assumes no responsibility for your actions.

Due to the dynamic nature of the Internet, any web addresses or links contained in this book may have changed since publication and may no longer be valid.

Henderson, Kim
Where Angels Fear to Tread: Finding Balance Through Breast Cancer / Kim Henderson – 1st ed.
ISBN: 978-0-6484729-0-2
1. Memoir. 2. Self-realisation. 3. Self-perception. 4. Self-discovery.

1st edition, February 2019.

Published by Kim Henderson
PO BOX 121, Stanhope Gardens NSW AUSTRALIA 2768
www.kimhenderson.com.au

Design by David Fleming
www.daf.id.au

Author photo by Belinda Walkom Photography
www.belindawalkom.com

For my family,
who fill my life with sunshine.

Contents

Introduction	11
Diagnosis	15
Waiting	37
Stress	45
Surgery	65
Recovery	81
Chemotherapy	95
Anxiety	119
Body Image	135
Nipples	151
Marriage	159
Menopause	165
Balance	171
Identity	185
References	195

My scars show my courage.
They are a sign of strength, not weakness.

Introduction

When I was first diagnosed with breast cancer, I felt like I was flying blind. Even though I had a strong support network and invaluable help from my family and friends, there were numerous times when I felt scared and alone. I struggled to make sense of the emotions that engulfed me.

The fear that arises out of a frightening diagnosis can be mentally and emotionally paralysing. It may feel like your whole world has been turned upside down and you're stuck in a dark and dismal place.

I hope this book will be a lifeline, something to aid you in your journey. In the midst of your suffering, when you are wondering, *Is what I'm feeling normal?*, I hope that my words—in all their gritty truth—will resonate with you and bring you comfort.

If you have found yourself on the precipice of a life-altering challenge, I want you to remember that you are not alone. Many others have walked this path where even angels fear to tread. I hope that my story will pave the way to make yours a little smoother.

Allow these pages to inspire you to find courage and resilience within yourself and help you through the mental and emotional upheaval you may experience, guiding you towards the development, improvement and expansion of your state of mind.

May you stride forward with grace and confidence, accepting what you must, but consciously blazing your own unique path. Do not allow fear to immobilise you, even when you believe it will. I hope that you will gain strength, insight, understanding and security from facing your fear.

I have learned that all it takes to negate fear is love. *Smother yourself in love.* Love yourself, with all your so-called flaws and imperfections, as deeply and as completely as you love another.

In sharing my story, I hope to help guide you towards finding the balance you are seeking.

Peace. Unity. Love.
Kim

INTRODUCTION

"I must not fear. Fear is the mind-killer."

— Frank Herbert, in *DUNE*

Diagnosis

Tuesday, 12th August

Have you ever sensed you were teetering on the edge of a life-altering experience? Troubled by the uneasy feeling of not being able to catch your breath? Or perhaps you've felt that nervous little knot of anxiety in your stomach letting you know that all is not quite right with the world…

Crap on a stick!

I have to go to the breast cancer clinic at the hospital. After my screening mammogram last month, I received a letter informing me that something was amiss with the results. The letter said an appointment had already been made for me.

It's today.

I have never been so *freaking* scared in my whole life. This has come entirely out of left-field. Having lost my mother to breast and metastatic brain cancer nine years ago, I am struck with absolute terror.

Since the moment I opened that letter, I have hardly slept or eaten. I wake up numerous times throughout the night, gripped with fear. I'm having terrible tummy problems—excruciating stomach pains and toilet urgency at all hours of the day and night. This is not the carefree life I'm used to leading as a busy mum to my two young boys.

My husband, James, has taken the day off work to come with me to the appointment. I try to convince myself that everything will be okay and that, because of Mum's cancer history, this is just an additional check-up to be extra careful.

We travel to the hospital, only a few suburbs away from our home. The irony is not lost on me that I am headed to the exact same clinic where Mum had been treated. As James steers the car into the parking lot, I vividly recall the many times I brought Mum here to attend her medical appointments. Powerful and unwelcome memories of struggling to entertain my then two-year-old son, while Mum had radiation treatment, begin frantically tugging at my mind like birds beating their wings against the bars of a cage.

We arrive at the consulting room and step into its cold

and clinical atmosphere. I try to be chirpy and act normal to mask my intense fear, all the while pretending this is a standard doctor's appointment with nothing to worry about.

I give my name to the receptionist, and almost immediately a nurse appears and leads me to a small change room to get clad in a hospital gown. The acrid smell of disinfectant hits my nostrils as we proceed to a sterile, white room. In the centre of the room is large metal mammography machine. My heart skips a beat as I realise I'm about to be tortured by its vice-like grip.

The nurse directs me to undress, and she inserts my right breast into the machine, taking x-ray after x-ray. Her examination is comprehensive and methodical.

I feel very uncomfortable. It is significantly more painful than my previous screening mammogram, and in considerably less-relaxing surroundings than the last, which I had done in the BreastScreen clinic behind the lingerie section of a department store. I think to myself, somewhat perversely, that there will be no cheerful shopping expedition at the conclusion of *this* examination.

Just when I think the torture is finally over, the nurse begins another more invasive mammogram from all different angles. By this stage, I am starting to freak out. I am cold, I am in pain, I am scared, and I feel incredibly lonely. The nurse is professional, but her manner is rather curt. How I would love for her to give me a friendly pat on the arm and tell me that everything will be okay.

After it's all over, the nurse leads me to a room where several other gowned women are seated. From the shell-shocked looks on some of their faces, I can clearly tell they have endured the same experience as me. The energy of the room feels as heavy as lead.

I feel like a product on a conveyor belt—just one of many worried women who has passed through this waiting room, amidst the looming threat of terrifying circumstances about to befall her. I try my hardest to think positively, quietly hoping that I will be given the all-clear and sent home shortly.

My eyes dart around the waiting room. One young woman flicks nonchalantly through a magazine, with the casual air of someone waiting at a bus stop. An older woman next to me weeps loudly, her sobs audible in the silent room. I begin talking to her in the hope it might offer some comfort. I try my best to give her some positive vibes, but I have to say, her fear is contagious, and I find myself faltering in my belief that all will be okay for both her and myself.

From the furtive glances I receive from the other women in the room, it is apparent that many of these ladies are fear-struck as well. I'll forever remember this room as 'The Waiting Room Of Terror'.

It occurs to me that there will only be two ways out

of here. Either the nurse will come in and tell me that the mammogram is clear and I can go on my merry way. *Or not.* The second option doesn't bear thinking about.

After an agonisingly long delay, the nurse calls my name and she advises that I'll need to have an ultrasound. Her demeanour is clinical and sombre, giving no indication of what to expect next. I begin to shiver, though it's more from fear than from the temperature of the room.

The nurse leads me to a darkened room and directs me to lay on a flat, sheet-covered bed. My mind starts to go woozy—I don't like where this is heading.

A young sonographer enters the room and introduces herself. After setting up the equipment and explaining the procedure, she runs the gel-covered transducer over my right breast.

"So, busy day huh?" I ask.

Silence.

"Have you seen any good movies lately?" I persist.

Her brow furrows with concentration as every attempt at small talk is met with stony silence. I immediately realise that something is wrong. *Incredibly wrong.*

With a gravely serious expression, the sonographer informs me that she needs to go and talk to the doctor. A wave of panic surges over me. I begin to tremble and my heart jackhammers in my chest. I feel light-headed and breathless at the same time. The unpleasant taste of vomit rises in the back of my throat, and my buttocks clench tightly as my fight-or-flight response kicks in. I try to calm myself by imagining God's hands reaching down and scooping me up to protect me.

My mind flashes back to when we visited the United States six months ago with our family friends, the Connells. We had booked a tour to go on the Skywalk at the West Rim of the Grand Canyon—a glass walkway built over the edge of the canyon, allowing tourists to peer down with an unobstructed view into the vast chasm below. There I was, standing at the edge of the transparent platform, with nothing but 600 metres of air between me and the floor of the Grand Canyon.

As my family coerced me into walking out across the glass to have a group photograph taken with our friends, I suddenly froze with fear as my panic grew. My breathing shortened to shallow, raspy gasps as I tried to resist my family's encouragement to step further out.

This experience was my own personal nightmare. The primal urge to flee was inescapable, but I was rooted to the spot, paralysed by fear. My inner voice screamed at me to back away, but my only movement was the trembling of my limbs as hot, salty tears streamed down my face.

It felt like the other tourists were all pointing and staring at me while I had this panic attack. This blessedly expensive excursion was wasted on me. The framed photo that I have of this event clearly shows the disparity of that day—everyone else is smiling excitedly while my face is frozen in a grimace of terror.

Lying here now, in this dark clinic room, I realise that, at that time, I had no idea what real fear was.

A lanky doctor breezes in and introduces himself. He takes a brief look at the ultrasound images on the computer screen and immediately says I need to have a biopsy. Actually, that I need to have two different biopsies. My head begins to swim. Everything seems fuzzy and surreal, like a fragmented dream sequence. My thoughts become haphazard and confused. *Is this really happening? Could I be dreaming?*

I begin to have what can only be described as an 'out-of-body experience'. As I look at this handsome doctor's face, his expression seems comical and exaggerated. His words don't make any sense to me at all. He may as well be speaking Swahili. I stammer out an unintelligible reply.

Concerned by my inability to respond, the nurse hurries out to fetch my husband. I begin hyperventilating and trembling violently. James arrives in a flash, and I am led to another room to have my vitals checked.

The doctors concur that I am not in any state to do the second biopsy as I would need to remain motionless throughout the procedure. They decide they will only do the core biopsy.

The words 'core biopsy' strike fear and dread into my heart. Even though I've had countless medical procedures in my life, including fertility treatment, which involved a *lot* of needles, the thought of a medical instrument, with a 'coring machine' at its end (yikes!) being inserted into my breast gives me the heebie-jeebies. The doctor administers a local anaesthetic, but it doesn't really cut the pain by any great measure. James holds my hand throughout the traumatic procedure, and his calming demeanour and loving eyes make me feel safe.

Arriving home after the biopsy, I feel sore and sorry for myself. My poor boob is extremely bruised, even after putting ice on it. Hopefully, it will feel better by morning.

I won't get the biopsy results until next Tuesday, a week from today. I have had better days.

Friday, 15th August

I've been trying so hard to think positively and forget about what is happening until my next appointment. My dear friend, Nicole, bought me a beautiful Tara Wolf bracelet. It is a symbol of the Flower of Life. The information card that came with it says:

The Flower of Life has deep spiritual meaning and is believed to contain the patterns of creation as they emerged from the Great Void. By meditating upon this symbol of Sacred Geometry and wearing the Flower of Life symbol on the body it has been known to have powerful healing benefits, helps to dissolve fears, assists in connecting to the higher self, stronger self-awareness and reveals the innate harmony in the template of all life.

This bracelet has become an amulet for me. I feel braver when I wear it, as if it is somehow safeguarding me from harm. I feel as though I need all the protection I can get at the moment.

I keep telling myself that lots of people go through this same experience. I am sure my results will turn out to be negative. Obviously I'm just keeping the doctors in business, otherwise they'd have nothing to do all day. I tell you what, I'm going to be cracking open a bottle of bubbly after I get the all-clear.

Tuesday, 19th August

Travelling to the hospital with James to get the results today is terrifying. I feel as though I am heading off to the gallows.

We arrive and the receptionist directs us to a small waiting room. This room is on the opposite side of the clinic to the one I sat in last week, only this time the wait to be called feels much longer.

I am extremely nervous. I can't even pick up a magazine. And I can't take my eyes off the pattern on the carpet. I swear that pattern will be imprinted on my brain for the rest of my life.

My thoughts are scattered. My legs are jittery. I can feel the little hairs on my arms stand on end in anticipation of what is to come.

I glance up as a white-coated figure enters the waiting room. It's the lovely female doctor who took my vitals the other day. As she looks toward me, I sense her hesitation to call my name.

I immediately know that it is *cancer*.

The doctor ushers us into a little examination room. I cannot comprehend the words coming out of her mouth. I look at James in desperation, but his eyes mirror the terror and grief in my own.

The doctor gives us some booklets on breast cancer and draws some diagrams about what this cancer is like, gently explaining I will need to have surgery to remove the tumour. Then she asks, "Who do you want as your surgeon?" I am astounded. *How the bloody hell should I know, lady?* I think to myself. I mean, it's not like I hang out on the medical scene, comparing surgeons for potential life-saving operations. I know she is only doing her job, but *sheesh!* I feel a horrendous sense of pressure. The glass is breaking, and I am falling through into the vast infinity of the Grand Canyon below.

The doctor scribbles down the names of a few different surgeons who specialise in breast cancer. I recognise one of them as the surgeon who operated on my mother. The familiarity of the name sparks a small glimmer of hope. We phone the surgeon's office, but I am disheartened to discover that the surgeon is on leave and cannot schedule me in for a few weeks. I suddenly feel lost and uncertain. The names on the list seem to blur together and I don't know how I can possibly make a decision.

The doctor then suggests we call my family physician to ask for her advice. My physician recommends a surgeon who happens to be the second name on the list, and I feel relieved that both doctors have agreed this surgeon would be the best one for me. It is the first time today that I've felt optimistic. The appointment is made for next Friday, ten days from now.

Walking out of the hospital is a surreal experience. My mind is spinning, I am sobbing, and people are staring. James grabs me by the elbow and steers me out of there as fast as he can.

Cancer? I can't fucking believe it!

This is so far out of my realm of understanding I can't

even comprehend it. I feel absolutely petrified. I am beside myself with worry. My mind hits fast-forward as I imagine every disastrous outcome I could possibly be facing. I don't know what to do first. I dread telling Dad this awful news. I can't fathom putting him through this again, not after what happened with Mum.

I phone my youngest brother, David, who has always been a calming influence in a crisis. Unexpectedly, he is at Dad's house, not far from the hospital. James and I drive straight there.

As we arrive at the house, I can't help but think about all the love I have experienced here at my childhood home. I run into Dad's arms, as I have done many times throughout my life, and I immediately feel secure, with a sense of hope that maybe, just maybe, I will be able to endure this.

Dad, David, James and I all sit glumly and stare at each other in shock. I phone my other brother, Anthony. He has recently welcomed a new baby into his family, so I am hesitant to share this terrible news with him and shatter his happiness. I remember back to when he had been living in Canada when our Mum phoned to tell him she had breast cancer. He was devastated he could not be by her side.

How could this happen to our family again? After losing our mother to cancer, it seems impossibly unfair that this menacing threat should rear its ugly head again.

DIAGNOSIS

I feel a looming sense of unease, anxiety and fear for the future. Panic sets in as I suddenly realise I have lost all control of my life. I'm 41 years old for Christ's sake! I'm in the prime of my life—fit, healthy and dedicated to raising my family. I eat healthy food. I exercise. I do karate twice a week with James and the boys. I don't smoke, I don't drink excessively, and I've never taken drugs. I even use natural body products, dammit! I am kind to others. I do my best to help people. I believe in God. *Why me?* Two little words that I begin to ask myself over and over again.

We drive home and wait for our sons, Nathaniel, aged 13, and Nicholas, 9, to arrive back from school. To pass the time, I browse through the booklet that the doctor had given me at the hospital: 'Talking to Kids about Cancer'. Who would have ever thought I'd have to discuss this with my kids at their young age? I've already decided to not hide anything from them. If I am open with them about everything and answer their questions honestly, it might be less frightening for them. I have always thought that trying to hide things from children makes them more worried. They can sense something is wrong when they overhear hushed conversations, and then their imaginations take hold, making the issue much scarier.

The boys arrive home, and we sit them down and gently tell them what is going on.

"Boys, we need to talk to you about something serious that is happening in our family," I say, my voice taking on an unnaturally high pitch.

Their adorable faces, eyes wide and innocent, turn expectantly to meet mine. For a moment I look at these precious children, and I am acutely aware that, even though they are young boys now, they will always be my babies. I want to protect them from all harm. I try to keep my voice from shaking. *Please, God, don't let me break down while I'm telling them this.*

"Mummy had to go to the doctor's for some tests today, and we found out that I have breast cancer. I will be going to the hospital so the doctors can operate on me to take the cancer away. But you don't need to worry. I'll be just fine."

Two sets of spindly little arms throw themselves around my neck and hug me tight. Nathaniel tries with all his might to blink back the tears that suddenly spring to his eyes.

They both know a bit about cancer from television, and from what I have told them regarding what happened to their grandmother. I try my best to explain that nothing much is going to change in their world—that there is nothing they need to be worried about. I tell them that we will be taking just as good care of them as we always have.

"The only change might be that Poppa may need to look after you if we are at doctor's appointments," I reassure them.

James asks the boys if they have any questions.

"Yeah! Can I go and play Xbox now?" Nicholas replies.

Nathaniel's brow knits together in concern as he asks, "Mummy, are you going to die?" I think carefully about my response.

"I have no plan on dying for a very, very long time, and I am going to do everything the doctors tell me, to make sure I'm around for a long time to come." It's my honest answer, and I hope it gives him some measure of comfort.

Nathaniel's question stirs uncomfortable feelings deep inside me. Truthfully, when I was told today that I had breast cancer, my absolute first thought was: *I'm going to die.* I am completely petrified. Dying is honestly my biggest fear. A fear I realise I will need to face.

We all seem to live our lives as if we are never going to die. In fact, it's like we all blindly believe we will live forever. Sometimes we think about our own death in an abstract kind of way, but until it's staring you in the face, it seems impossible to imagine.

Facing your own mortality is something that we will all have to do, eventually. But it's one of those things that we seem to push to the back of our minds, denying the eventuality until such time, always in the much later future, that we will actually have to think about it.

Being in this situation now, forced to suddenly confront

the prospect of death in a very real way, is deeply troubling.

Despite my intense fear, I do, however, plan on trying my best to be positive, open and honest with my kids throughout the whole process and during my cancer treatment, whatever that may end up being. It's my responsibility as their mother to support them through this distressing time, and I will try my best to quell their fears.

I hope that I will be able to show them that, sometimes, horrible things happen in life, but we don't have to let them destroy us. Together, as a family, we can face this thing and hopefully emerge as an even stronger family unit.

People often speak in hushed terms around someone who is going through a dire illness or challenging event in their life. I think it's better to get everything out in the open. It seems to be less scary that way.

When I was growing up, I remember how open and honest Mum was about any problem that occurred in our family. As a teenager, it annoyed me no end that our seemingly private family matters were discussed in the open arena of our extended family and friends. However, as I grew into an adult, I came to see her purpose in doing this. Mum knew that if you bring your problems out into the open, they seem to shrink and become much less overwhelming.

When we talk about our issues and seek guidance from family and trusted friends, we can gain the emotional support we need to solve our dilemma. We should all share our problems and concerns in order to diminish them.

Wednesday, 20th August

Sleep evades me. Why does everything seem much worse at 3:00 a.m.? I reach across the bed for James' hand under the covers. He holds my hand tightly. I know that, with him by my side, I can get through anything.

My dear friend, Louise, is coming to visit, so that will be a nice distraction. She has been like a sister to me since we first met, when we were both fresh, young newly-weds, living next door to each other.

Louise is the best kind of friend to have in a crisis. She is a decisive, no-nonsense person with critical thinking skills. She has been through many challenges in her own life, including losing both her parents to illness, so I know she will help me feel stronger today.

I've felt some moments of intense anger about my situation. The anger appears to be serving some purpose though, giving me the strength to fight this.

I am reminded of the Kübler-Ross model of grief[1] I learned about at school, which applies to many situations, including the onset of disease or chronic illness:

> DENIAL – *The first reaction is denial. In this stage, individuals believe the diagnosis is somehow mistaken, and cling to a false, preferable reality.*

Yep, been there. I've already imagined a scenario in my mind many times where the doctor tells me they've made a mistake and, in fact, it's not cancer. I end up skipping out of the doctor's surgery on cloud nine.

> ANGER – *When the individual recognises that denial cannot continue, they become frustrated, especially at proximate individuals. Certain psychological responses of a person undergoing this phase would be: "Why me? It's not fair!"; "How can this happen to me?"; "Who is to blame?"; "Why would this happen?"*

Again, yes! It's like I wrote this one! The anger strikes when I least expect it. I lash out at God and the Universe, screaming into my pillow and crying tears of rage. Looking for a source of blame seems natural, even though, on some level, I realise how unhelpful this is.

I am ashamed to admit it but, the other day I was feeling especially stressed out waiting for my results when, without warning, a woman abruptly and selfishly drove in front of my car, nearly causing an accident. I flew into a white-hot fury like never before in my life. I shrieked obscenities out of the window. Thank goodness my kids weren't in the car. I honestly felt like dragging that poor woman out of her car and screaming in her face, "DON'T YOU REALISE WHAT I'M GOING THROUGH?"

> BARGAINING – *The third stage involves the hope that the individual can avoid a cause of grief. Usually, the negotiation for an extended life is made in exchange for a reformed lifestyle. People facing less serious trauma can bargain or seek compromise.*

Believe me, I have bargained with God, promising Him so many things that, when this is over, I will be working for the rest of my life to achieve them all.

> DEPRESSION – *"I'm so sad, why bother with anything?"; "I'm going to die soon, so what's the point?"; "I miss my loved one, why go on?" During the fourth stage, the individual despairs at the recognition of their mortality. In this state, the individual may become silent, refuse visitors and spend much of the time mournful and sullen.*

So far I have managed to escape this one, but it sounds all too familiar.

I distinctly remember Mum suffering from such a deep depression after she was diagnosed with metastatic brain cancer. I was present at the surgery with Mum and Dad when the doctor spoke those dreadful words to her: "Go home and put your affairs in order." The three of us were utterly speechless.

By the time we arrived home, I was all fired up, planning ways to seek out alternative routes for healing—unorthodox treatments that were just beginning to emerge during the early stages of the Internet. But my poor mother took to her bed and stayed there for weeks on end. We couldn't entice her to take joy in anything.

I remember being angry with her because I thought she was wasting her final, precious moments. I sorely wanted her to spend some quality time with my son, Nathaniel, her only grandchild at that time, so he would have some treasured memories of his beloved *Nanna*. I was sure his cute little face could deliver her out of depression, but it was not to be.

I didn't understand what she was going through. I was young and *gung-ho*. I believed we could beat this!

Looking back, I feel selfish in my response to her depression, but I honestly didn't understand her emotional state, and I couldn't fathom the depth of her despair.

The last stage of the Kübler-Ross model is:

ACCEPTANCE – *"It's going to be okay."; "I can't fight it; I may as well prepare for it." In this last stage, individuals embrace mortality or inevitable future, or that of a loved one, or other tragic event. People dying may precede the survivors in this state, which typically comes with a calm, retrospective view for the individual, and a stable condition of emotions.*

I reflect on the many trials that my family and I have dealt with. We were devastated when we lost Mum to cancer at the age of fifty-five. We suffered the shattering loss of Dad's youngest brother in a horrific plane crash. I've endured the devastating emotional consequences of infertility and the harsh physical and emotional effects of IVF treatment. Our first son was born eight weeks prematurely. I have experienced so much pain, heartache and loss in my life that I solemnly ponder whether I am strong enough to face this new challenge.

"Courage is knowing what not to fear."

— Plato

Waiting

Thursday, 21st August

Life, whether we realise it or not, is filled with tasks. We seem to focus almost purely on getting the next thing done. Then the next thing. And the next. We get busy *doing*. Busy begins to feel normal. This leads to feeling unappreciated and can breed resentment, especially between partners. It can become a vicious spiral into discontent.

Sometimes, I feel like my dreams of what I wanted my life to be like have faded. What started off as a fairytale has become mundane. I have been so busy *doing* that I have completely forgotten about *being*. Life seems to have hurried by while I've mindlessly repeated the same behaviours and reactions without critical thought—wash, rinse, repeat—and I've lulled myself into a false sense of security that this is life—it just goes on. Until one day it doesn't.

"Stop and smell the roses," remember that old chestnut? Waiting here now on this cliff-edge of fear and dread to find out what my future holds—if I even have a future at all—I wish, with all my heart that I did, in fact, stop and smell those damn roses.

Friday, 22nd August

We are heading off to meet our friends for our annual snow-skiing holiday. James and I both decide we need to keep up our normal life, even though it feels like we are in the eye of an incredibly vast hurricane.

While travelling in the car, I notice a huge rainbow that seems to fill the entire sky, and I suddenly experience an intense moment of serenity.

I wonder how many rainbows I have ignored, always rushing to get to the next place and do the next thing. I will never forget this breathtaking vision, and I promise myself that I will slow down and enjoy each rainbow. As the saying goes, "You can't have a rainbow without a little rain," so I need to appreciate the rain too.

We are staying in the most beautiful chalet in the snow,

built from rough-hewn stone. Inside, it is warm and comfy, with a couple of cosy fireplaces and a welcoming bar, complete with mulled wine. It almost feels like I'm in the French Alps. However, it is the strangest sensation being here in this ordinary social setting and knowing that I have cancer.

I feel like an outsider. *A freak.* I can sense the tension in the air as my friends make small talk, avoiding the elephant in the room. No one seems to know what to say to me. I guess they don't want to upset me by asking too many questions. And I don't blame them, I can hardly talk to anyone without dissolving into tears anyway. I feel despondent and more alienated than ever. I realise, sadly, that I must go through this experience alone. No one can experience it *for* me.

I think of all the times when I have tried to help friends through their crises. I recognise now that I have always mistakenly believed that it was my responsibility to cheer them up or cajole them into looking at the bright side of life. That's the technique I used when dealing with Mum's illness. I always felt compelled to point out someone who was in a worse position than her. I tried to force her to see the positive side of her situation. I didn't understand at the time that this would have been no help to her at all.

I now realise that the most beneficial thing is to just *be* there with that person in their time of need. Not to try and fix it for them or cheer them up, or to point out how much unluckier they might have been. Instead, to be fully present in that moment with them. To show them how much you care by telling them that, although you honestly have no idea what they're going through, you are there for them in any way, shape or form that they need you to be.

It's now clear to me that sometimes, you just have to sit with someone and feel their pain and sadness, in order to help take some of it away.

Saturday, 23rd August

We finish hiring our ski gear and paying for the kids' ski school when our youngest son, Nicholas, unexpectedly begins vomiting with such violence that I swear his head is about to start spinning around.

James and I both get covered in puke, and we stand dumbfounded for a few moments, not knowing how to begin cleaning it up. Trust this to happen! Nicholas hadn't even complained about feeling sick. Our holiday has barely begun, and I'm ready to turn around and go home.

A short while later Nicholas declares he feels fine and wants to go to ski school after all. We venture outside, and Nicholas joins the gang of merry children, laughing and playing in the snow. He doesn't want me to leave him, in case he gets sick again, so I abandon my plans of skiing for the day. I assure James that I will be perfectly fine and send him off to the slopes. I want him to try and have some fun on this holiday to relieve the pressure he must be feeling after dealing with all of our family drama. Besides, it's no use wasting both our ski passes.

I take a seat inside the roped-off parent's area, covered in vomit and watch my son play in the distance—a brightly coloured dot against the backdrop of brilliant white snow.

All I want is a hot shower to wash the vomit off my clothes and get the pungent smell out of my hair. Coffee would be nice too. This is the *worst* holiday ever!

After what seems like hours out in the cold, the kids and I head back to the chalet, and I finally get to have that longed-for shower. I am proud that Nicholas stuck it out all day at ski school. He seems to have had an enjoyable day after all.

While the kids settle down to watch television in our room, I venture out to see if I can spot James coming back from the slopes. I pass a young man waiting outside the front door of the chalet. He couldn't be more than twenty years old. And he happens to be in a wheelchair.

We start chatting, and I learn that one year prior, he had been involved in a motorcycle accident which left him permanently paralysed from the waist down. I discover that he is the son of the lodge owners, who had purchased the chalet only weeks before his accident. He describes what it was like having his whole life change in an instant, expressing with heartfelt emotion the challenges he has had to face. He explains the difficulty of adjusting to life in a wheelchair, dealing with the grief of losing his mobility and having to regain his confidence and find new ways to live again. He shares his story so matter-of-factly, and without any self-pity, it brings me to tears. Despite having endured a tragedy that has obviously been a life-changing experience for both himself and those that love him, he appears to have fully accepted the situation and adapted to his new life.

I tell him about being diagnosed with cancer. He expresses genuine concern, in such an empathetic way, which I find astonishing for someone so young. Perhaps the life challenges he has faced at such an early age have given him a deep understanding of the feelings of others.

His mates soon arrive in their over-snow vehicle, and he heads out for a night on the town.

I am in awe of this remarkable human being. Although our conversation was brief, this young man truly inspires me. Meeting someone with an attitude of total acceptance and peacefulness toward the difficult circumstances he found himself in, strengthens my resolve to handle my own situation in a more positive manner.

This man appears to be living life purposefully, and with apparent vigour, making the most of every single day.

What the hell do I have to worry about? I only have cancer. I am lucky enough to live in a country where we have access to world-leading experts in advanced and specialised medical care for cancer patients. I'm not living in a third world country, where having any kind of illness could be a death sentence. No, we can't cure cancer yet, but we sure as hell have an arsenal of treatments at our disposal. I know how lucky I am. This young man has to live the whole of his life facing challenges that I could not even begin to imagine.

In one remarkable moment, this unique and beautiful soul shared his story with me, and I was given a glimpse that I too can experience acceptance of *all that is*.

*"In all chaos there is a cosmos,
in all disorder a secret order."*

— Carl Jung

Stress

Wednesday, 27th August

Far out! I've just started bleeding mid-cycle. This has never happened before. It's hard not to worry when you see blood, and you know you shouldn't. What else could go wrong?

I do what every woman does when something unusual happens to her body—I Google it.

'Doctor Google' suggests that stress can cause mid-cycle bleeding. And menopause! What the…? As if I don't already have enough on my mind. Why did this have to happen today? I phone my doctor, who sends me for an immediate pelvic ultrasound.

After driving to the clinic for the scan and waiting for what seemed like an extraordinarily long time for the results, I am greatly relieved to find out there is nothing seriously wrong, except for what appears to be an ovarian cyst. Thankfully, it's nothing to worry about. The sonographer isn't sure what caused the bleeding but said it can be common.

I have lost a lot of weight over these past two weeks, and I'm not eating or sleeping well. Everything is so messed up right now. I just don't feel like *myself*. The weather appears to mimic my mood: grey, depressing and miserable.

I've never been much of a crier, yet these days I dissolve into tears every five minutes. It's quite exhausting. Bubbling to the surface of my mind is a lot of fear and sadness related to Mum's death, which I now realise I have not adequately dealt with. Crying seems to be my way of processing what has happened, enabling me to release the emotions I've been carrying around for so many years.

I remember back to when Mum underwent her initial surgery. She was positive and uplifting to everyone she interacted with—the doctor, the nurses and visitors. She was much braver than me. I feel defeated and scared. I desperately wish I still had Mum by my side to help me through this. I miss her more than ever.

James has been a bit of a mess this past week too. His *go-to* emotion whenever he feels out of control is anger. He's been getting angry at the smallest and most inane things lately. Seriously, the world isn't going to end if one of the kids leaves the lights on in their room, or forgets to load their plate into the dishwasher! Thankfully, he has been receiving support from Dad, who has allowed him a safe space to express his fears and emotions. Some good mates of his have also called in for a beer and a chat to help take his mind off things.

James has never been a very demonstrative man, preferring to keep his emotions in check, but lately, he has shown a whole new side.

We've been talking a lot about what lies ahead, and he has been especially supportive and caring. James is extremely considerate of my feelings, choosing his words carefully when we talk, and he has reassured me that he won't care how my body will look after surgery, especially if I need to have a mastectomy. His compassion and ability to express his love to me in every deed makes me realise how deeply I love and cherish this man.

As well as being a supportive and loving husband, James is quite practical as well. He vacuums the floors *constantly*, which drives me mad, but I understand it helps make him feel more in control if our house is clean and tidy.

We endeavour to find something to laugh about every single day, and we try our hardest to see the joy in life, however small. We have been watching funny movies in our spare time. Our favourite is the *American Pie* series of films. Watching Seann William Scott play 'Stifler', with his uncensored antics, never fails to have us in hysterics. We also love watching Jim Carey in his *Ace Ventura: Pet Detective* movies. I swear that man was put on Earth solely to make people laugh and forget about their problems for a while.

I am going to cook a batch of meals and freeze them to have on hand, in case I don't have the time or energy to make dinner while I am recovering from surgery. Having nutritious meals to grab out of the freezer will take a lot of the pressure off. I wish James had learned to cook before now. *Note to self: teach our sons to cook!* Getting organised about the practicalities of how the house is going to run while I'm out of action seems to ease my nerves.

I am anxious about meeting the breast cancer surgeon later this week to decide what surgical option I will take. Last week, the diagnosing doctor at the hospital told me that my choices were either a lumpectomy, where they only partially operate on the breast to remove the tumour, and some surrounding tissue, followed by radiation treatment; or I can choose to have a mastectomy, which may negate the need for radiation therapy. How do I know what will be the right decision for me?

Having watched Mum go through breast cancer surgery is the only frame of reference I have to go by. She had a lumpectomy, but the pathology results indicated that the surgeons didn't get clear margins—enough cancer-cell-free area around the tumour—so she had to go back a week later for more surgery, this time to have a full mastectomy.

I don't want to take what initially seems like the easier path, only to end up back on the surgeon's table again.

I've been talking to a friend of mine who was diagnosed with breast cancer twelve years ago when she was just 31 years old. She had a single mastectomy followed by radiation treatment and chemotherapy. She still has to have a mammogram every year on her remaining breast which, she told me, is a bit of a chore and something that always causes her to feel anxious.

I'm leaning towards having a double mastectomy because I can't imagine going through this terror again. The past few weeks have been horrifying enough as it is and I know I would not cope well if I had to face this situation twice.

I am also very big busted—a size E cup in my bras. I know this sounds completely vain, given the gravity of the situation, but I can't help worrying I'd be left lopsided with only one breast.

I've heard stories, which seem funny in an awkward kind of way, about women's breast prostheses falling out during swimming or exercise. I don't think that's something I could handle very well. I'd rather have no breasts at all. Think of all the active things I'd be able to do without my big boobs getting in the way. Maybe I could take up jogging! I must look on the bright side!

Friday, 29th August

I finally get to meet my surgeon. He is charming, and his gentle manner immediately puts my mind at ease. He is especially patient with me, describing all of my options in great detail.

He explains that, because I have large breasts, and with the amount of breast tissue I would need to have removed in a lumpectomy, I would end up being very lopsided. He suggests that, if I decided to go for this option, I should also have a breast reduction on the other side to match. This does not appeal to me at all. If I'm going to need to have surgery on both breasts, I'd rather have them both gone. Then I won't ever have to fear getting cancer in the other breast. All I want is to get this cancer out of my body.

One of the things I wonder most about is: *what will happen with my nipples?*

I recently read that the actress, Angelina Jolie, had a 'nipple-sparing preventative mastectomy'. The name of this surgery simultaneously intrigued and horrified me.

During this procedure, the nipple—which has been receiving its blood supply from the breast tissue—is surgically removed and later grafted back onto the muscle and breast skin. It then has to try and develop a brand new blood supply. Even if it did successfully adhere, it wouldn't have any feeling and wouldn't look the same as it did originally.

My surgeon explains he doesn't usually like to preserve the nipple on the breast that has cancer because the malignant cells can travel through the milk ducts towards the nipple. So, although it's possible to keep the nipple, I may run the risk of cancer recurring in the future. *No thanks.*

Besides, as the surgeon informs me, nipple preservation complicates the surgery and increases the risk of infection.

After weighing up the surgical options, I am relieved to make the decision to have a 'bilateral skin-sparing mastectomy'. This means I will be having both of my breasts surgically removed.

The surgeon will operate to remove the breast tissue while retaining the skin covering the breasts, allowing me to have an immediate breast reconstruction with small silicone implants.

The surgeon explains that having this type of reconstructive surgery will negate the need for tissue expanders and further surgery later. The possibility of this type of surgery had not even crossed my mind as an option, so I am thrilled that, post-mastectomy, I will look closer to my usual self when clothed. My surgeon also explains that I will probably need to have chemotherapy down the track as well.

I wonder how I'll feel about my body after this surgery? I'm trying hard to focus on the positives. No more stiff nipples on cold days! And getting implants—fancy that. At least I won't have to tuck my saggy boobs into my pants when I'm old!

My operation is booked for next Thursday, six days from now. I will be in hospital for at least four nights, with an eight-week recovery period at home after that. I won't be able to lift my arms above my head or drive a car for a couple of months, so I am going to need a lot of physical help.

James and I were worried about the cost of the surgery. As luck would have it, we only took out a private health insurance policy one year ago yesterday. We've never been able to budget well enough to afford private medical cover, and I couldn't see the point since we were seemingly fit and healthy.

Call it a premonition, but that decision to sign up for health insurance is something I am incredibly grateful for right now.

I phone the health insurance company to make sure I am covered for the surgery. Luckily I've just scraped in.

Although I am confident I would have received the same level of care through the public hospital system, having private cover allows me not only to choose my surgeon, but also where I'll go to have chemotherapy. We will still be several thousand dollars out of pocket, but fortunately we have a little bit of money saved up. *Goodbye island holiday.*

James will need to take two or three weeks off work after my surgery to care for me and run the household. Financially it is going to be tricky because he is a sub-contractor and won't be getting paid while not at work. He is not entitled to paid sick leave or even paid holiday leave. My part-time job is only casual, so I will be without an income until I can physically work again.

I had never thought about the financial impact an illness like cancer could have on our family. I feel as though I have been caught off guard, but then again, I don't know of too many couples with young families and a mortgage who are financially prepared in case of accident or illness.

I wish I had listened more carefully to those advertisements on television about taking out income protection insurance. That might have come in handy now!

My friend, Nicole, gave me a great big belly laugh today. She recalled the time her husband went to hospital for a hip operation. He was so worried the doctors might operate on the wrong side that he stuck a Band-Aid on his hip with the words 'THIS ONE' written on it in black marker. Too funny! Thank goodness I don't have to worry about them doing the wrong side. I say take them both and give me a set of perky new ones!

I dug out a t-shirt that was given to me many years ago by my Canadian friend, Joanna, who shares my perverse sense of humour. The print on the front reads, 'I used up all my sick days, so I called in dead'. I've decided I'm wearing it to surgery. Maybe it will give the doctors and nurses a laugh.

Sunday, 31st August

My lifelong friend, Melinda, sent me an uplifting message today. It was exactly what I needed to hear.

...

Kim, I just want to say I have a really good feeling this is going to be a blip in your life. What doesn't kill you makes you stronger, right?

I feel happy to know you have strong support from James. You are two peas in a pod with your sense of humour and outlook. I know he will look out for you.

When you need to let it all out, you can unload to us. Anytime you need help, or someone to talk to, we're always here for you. You will never be alone.

I know the next few weeks and months are going

STRESS

to be tough, but you are a survivor, and this experience will make you stronger.

By summer you'll be sitting by the pool in your bikini looking at your new boobs, wine in hand and thinking, 'how great is this!' and then the boys will start fighting, and life will be back to normal.

...

I received another message from a dear childhood friend and journalist, Kate.

...

Life will never be the same—but there's a real good chance it will be better.

In my experience of interviewing survivors, many find they enjoy life more after cancer. They also discover, within themselves, a resilience they never knew they had.

You *will* get there. Acknowledge the fears at 3:00 a.m. and maybe you can write them down, or even send them to us so we can help you deal with them. This will also give you a chance to process them in the light of day. Maybe once you write them down, you can get back to sleep, which you really need.

You got onto this early, and you will beat it. I just know that to be true.

...

Thank God for my friends. They are treasures. I have drawn so much strength from being able to talk to them, and their positivity lifts me up so high.

I've been thinking about giving an amusing name to this operation: 'Boob Voyage', 'The Pointer Sisters Farewell Tour' or 'Ta-ta to the Tatas'. It's important to me to try and bring light to this experience and find the funny side!

Dad had made me a big blackboard for my kitchen which I use to plan our family's weekly schedule. I've bravely written on it in big, bold letters for Thursday: 'BOOB VOYAGE'.

Monday, 1st September

I have been trying to live a normal life while I wait for surgery—doing the grocery shopping, cleaning the house and completing the chores. To break the monotony, I've decided to visit my friend, Mel, for a coffee. Maybe I'll gain a little slice of normality in this extremely abnormal situation.

Mel and I first met at the hospital when Nathaniel was

three weeks old. He was born prematurely and had been transferred from the neonatal intensive care unit to the special care nursery. Mel's baby, Taylah, had also been admitted to the nursery, after suffering complications during her birth.

I'll never forget seeing Mel for the first time, limping into the nursery, having just given birth the night before. There I was, all perky and cheerful, having recovered from the birth experience by then, smiling empathetically at the way she gingerly tried to sit down on the chair next to me. We struck up a conversation and discovered that we lived on the same street.

Although she has since moved house, we have remained the best of friends. We each fell pregnant with our second children at exactly the same time, having our babies only six days apart. Our kids have grown up together, and we've shared many cherished, and often hilarious, moments together. Mel is one of those friends I know I can turn to when I need a good laugh.

During the short drive over to her house, I am suddenly overcome with a feeling of complete desperation. I feel sick, anxious and despondent all at once. I can't breathe. I am choking on a massive chunk of emotion that has become lodged in my throat.

I am drowning, frantically trying to claw my way back up to the surface of my normal life. I am so overwhelmed that

I pull the car over to the side of the road, take a few deep breaths and choke back the tears.

I try desperately to understand the depth of what I am feeling and why I have suddenly been overcome with emotion. I decide to name the feeling to try and make some sense of it. The word I come up with for the emotion is 'despair'. I couldn't possibly sink any lower than this. This is the lowest of the low—the pits. The only way I am going to be able to move past this feeling is to feel it fully. To let go and jolly well *feel* it, instead of denying it.

I begin talking out loud to myself, "Okay, right now I am experiencing total and utter despair. This is what despair feels like. It is horrible. I don't think I've ever felt so low in my life. This is certainly an experience of being in total misery. If, sometime in the future, someone says to me they are in despair, I will completely understand what they mean. Okay, I've fully embraced that emotion of despair now. It's time to move on. Goodbye 'despair'."

As I arrive at Mel's house, a deep peacefulness washes over me. A tiny flicker of hope sparks in my mind, it's embers fanned by the flames of relief and, somehow, I know that 'despair' is an emotion that will never gain control over me again.

Tuesday, 2nd September

I've been trying on all my bras and photographing myself. I laugh as I imagine what would happen if these selfies accidentally uploaded to the cloud like in the Cameron Diaz movie *Sex Tape!* These photos are definitely not for publishing.

I don't know if I'm just weird, or if other women facing a mastectomy have considered photographing their breasts before surgery. My boobs have been with me for, well, as long as I can remember. I want to be able to look back on these photographs and remember what they were like.

It's going to be strange—I am literally having my breasts cut off. It's *bloody* scary!

I wonder if, after the operation, I will look at myself and feel like I've been maimed and mutilated? I'm terrified of being disfigured, and I am scared I'll no longer have any feeling in my chest.

My breasts have simultaneously been both a blessing and a curse. A blessing in the way they have made me feel good about myself—they have always made me feel womanly. And a blessing in that they enabled me to feed and bond with my babies. I kept my children nourished and alive with only my breasts. That's no mean feat!

Conversely, my breasts have also been a curse, often interfering with the things I want to do, like running or wearing certain styles of clothing—I have never been able to go braless or wear strappy dresses like women with smaller busts. And now within them, I carry this wretched cancer. I feel like my breasts have let me down.

I'm finding that I want to involve my breasts in lovemaking with James as much as I can, kind of like giving them a farewell—one last *hurrah*. I wonder if other women in this situation have ceremoniously farewelled their breasts in this way? James is such a good man—I'm sure it's the very last thing he feels like doing, but he is so gentle, loving and considerate of my needs.

I've been recording my thoughts and feelings, my highs and lows, in a small diary that I keep beside the bed. It's strange, but ever since I visited the breast cancer clinic, the same thought keeps popping into my mind: *Does my future somehow involve helping other people face this scary thing?*

There is definitely not enough emotional support available when you first get diagnosed. It feels as though they just tell you, "You have cancer," and send you home. There's a lot of waiting around with no one to talk to about what's going to happen. If I didn't have the support of my family and friends, I think my anxiety levels would have been a lot more pronounced.

Wouldn't it be great if, from day one, the doctors put you in touch with at least one support person, preferably some-

STRESS

one who has been through a similar diagnosis and treatment and, hopefully, someone who is positive and uplifting.

I feel sorry for all the women in this situation who don't have the support that I am fortunate enough to have. Being able to vent to my family and friends in a non-judgemental space has saved me from losing the plot, emotionally and mentally.

The breast care nurse, whom I saw at the surgeon's office, told me that I could see a psychologist if I needed to, but the waiting list was quite long. This is outrageous! Surely mental health assistance should be easily accessible to people who have been diagnosed with cancer?

I've never needed to seek professional help with regards to my mental state before, but gosh, I reckon it would do me some good now!

Wednesday, 3rd September

Last night our youngest son, Nicholas, became terribly sick. We battled all night to get his temperature below forty degrees Celsius. James slept on the floor next to his bed to keep an eye on him.

Early this morning, we raced him up to our local doctor, who suspected pneumonia and sent him straight to the x-ray clinic for chest imaging. The doctor told us that if the x-ray showed his chest was too full of congestion, he would need to be admitted to hospital. Well, I completely lost it. *God help us!*

While James is with Nicholas at the clinic, I hurry to the chemist to get the antibiotic prescription filled. We start Nicholas on his medication as soon as we get home. I am stressed, upset and crying with worry.

I begin packing a hospital bag, when the phone suddenly rings. It's our doctor, who advises that Nicholas has pneumonia in both lungs. Fortunately, she feels we will be able to manage it at home on the strong medication, as long as he rests and stays warm.

What a day! I now understand the meaning of the proverb, "It never rains, but it pours."

Dad calls in to sit with Nicholas while James takes me to the hospital to have some tests in preparation for my surgery tomorrow.

The first test is to see how fast the lymph fluid travels through my system. The second one involves having four, extremely painful needles inserted directly into my nipple and breast, and a radioactive dye injected into the tumour to see which lymph nodes it drains to. This is only slightly less terrible than I imagined it would be—it stings like hell!

Before I've had a chance to feel sorry for myself, I am whisked off to another room and directed to lie on a narrow examination table in front of a CT scanner—a huge doughnut-shaped device. A nurse covers me with a blanket, and the table glides smoothly into the machine. There is a slight humming sound, followed by a whirring sound as the X-ray tube rotates around me. I begin to feel very alone and scared.

As my mind wanders, the magnitude of this situation suddenly hits. I've been so busy rushing around like crazy for the past few days, from one thing to the next, that I've not stepped back to look at the bigger picture. The road ahead suddenly seems incredibly daunting. I have an operation to undergo, with weeks of recovery afterwards, potential chemotherapy to endure, a household to maintain, a sick child at home...

...And my surgery day is tomorrow.

*"Truly, it is in darkness that one finds the light,
so when we are in sorrow,
then this light is nearest of all to us."*

— Meister Eckhart

Surgery

Thursday, 4th September

Last night was tough. I was so anxious with worry about the operation that I barely slept.

I have undergone a number of surgeries before—laparoscopies, a D&C, an open reduction on a broken shoulder—but this one genuinely scares me. For the first time in my life, I am absolutely petrified that I will not survive this day.

The doctor told me it will be a long and challenging surgery with two teams working simultaneously on either side of my body for around six hours. *God, please help me get through this.*

I secretly wrote letters to my husband and sons last night.

Should I die during the surgery today, I hope they will later discover those letters and know I was thinking only of them.

...

To James, my Darling Husband, my one true love, my soul mate.

We are one throughout eternity. You are the air I breathe, the water I drink. You are the sunshine that brightens my day. You are my *everything*. Your strength gives me the courage to face life each day in every way.

When I was a little girl, I dreamed of marrying a tall, dark and handsome man. I dreamed of you. We were destined by fate.

The moment I knew we would be together forever was on our first weekend spent waterskiing together. I was in the back of your boat, you were driving, shirtless and suntanned. I have that exact photo of you, looking back over your shoulder at me, smiling. I could foresee our children in your eyes. I drank in the sight of you—carefree, happy and perfect.

You have made me feel like a princess since the day we married. I treasure those early years when it was just you and me against the world. Yes, we had some hard times, but they only served to make us stronger and cement our ties.

You gave me the ultimate gift—two amazing sons in the exact likeness of you. They are both so much like you in mannerisms and personality. To see the three of you laughing together is the best sight in the world.

I love you all so much. More than you could ever imagine. I know we will always be together, in the next life and the next.

I love you.

...

To my beautiful, first-born son, Nathaniel.

Do you know I loved you before I even met you, when you were just a 'jelly bean' in my tummy?

I loved that being pregnant with you made me crave popcorn. I knew that you would have a preference for salty food. I talked to you every day in my belly, and when you started to arrive early, I was so scared I would lose you. You were our precious gift from God, as your name implies.

Your early days were traumatic, but you were

resilient. I knew you were a fighter because you were just like Daddy and me. You never gave up. You grew big and strong.

Taking you home from hospital five weeks before the doctors estimated was extraordinary. Daddy drove the car like he had a dozen loose eggs on the back seat.

Those early days at home with just you and me were bliss. You were the perfect baby, and you ate and became chubby and cute. We took you everywhere with us so you could experience all the wonders of the world.

I tried so hard to be the perfect mother. Sometimes I felt I had failed you, especially when I was so down and depressed after your Nanna died. I used to kiss your forehead at night-time while you slept and apologise for not being perfect—I would try harder tomorrow. I hope that I was still able to create happy memories for you during those difficult days.

You are growing up to be such a perfect young man. You make me so proud with your excellent manners, intelligence, confidence and especially your wicked sense of humour! My wish for you is that you will stay true to yourself, do what *you* want to do, stay on your own path and try to find joy in every day.

SURGERY

Never be afraid of life. The world is an amazing, wonderful place and you will always be protected.

I love you always,
Mummy.

...

To my dearest, darling, precious son Nicholas, you'll always be my baby.

I felt your spirit at Christmastime before you were even conceived. Natty, Daddy and I were putting up the Christmas tree in the lounge room when I sensed your presence. I even told Daddy that a new baby would be coming into our family shortly. He didn't believe me!

We were over the moon when we found out you were in my tummy. Natty told me early on that you would be a boy—he just knew.

We talked to you every day. You were obviously very cosy in there because you didn't want to come out. Finally, after a day of gardening in 40-degree heat at your Nanna and Poppa's house, one week after you were due, you decided to make your arrival.

Nanna was there to see you being born too. I will

never forget the way you blinked your eyes like a newborn kitten in the sunshine of the delivery room.

You loved to be held. You were never happy unless you were in my arms.

As a toddler, you were my cheeky monkey, always inquisitive and independent.

"Go away, Mummy! Me do!" you would call out. Daddy and I thought you were the cutest little cherub in the world.

When you were five months old, your Nanna died, and I was very sad. I hope this didn't affect you too much. I tried very hard to be there for you.

Do you know I still sit for ages staring at you and kissing your perfect, cherubic cheeks while you are asleep?

I think you are brilliant. I am in awe of your intelligence, and already, at 9 years old, I can see the gentleman you will become. You have a spark about you that I just love.

Please, just be yourself. Don't worry about what other people think. You need to be happy in yourself. You need to make *you* happy.

Channel your natural nervousness into powering you forward in life. Nothing can go wrong—you will always be protected.

SURGERY

My funny little boy, I love you more than all the strawberries in the world.

Love you always,
Mummy.

...

Arriving at the hospital is the strangest feeling. Again, it is like I am having an out-of-body experience. Everything seems surreal and out of focus. Could I really be doing this? Is this really happening to me? This is so far from any reality I have ever experienced before.

Why, oh why, can't this just be a typical day of making the lunches, seeing my kids off to school and going to work? What I would give to be having an uneventful day, where the most exciting thing I had planned to do was the ironing, or some other mundane and ordinary task.

I check in at the admissions desk, and James and I are asked to wait in a huge room full of people sitting in rows of chairs lined up facing a television.

Down one side of the room is a corridor with lots of doors leading from it. One of the doors opens, and I can see inside to a tiny room with a desk and a chair.

A nurse steps out from the room holding a clipboard.

Almost everyone waiting turns toward her expectantly as she calls a name. A woman sitting nearby shifts nervously in her seat. She stands up, gathers her things and proceeds to the door. It closes behind her with an ominous *thud*.

After ten minutes, the same nurse emerges from behind the door and calls another name. As I watch each patient enter this room and not return, it perversely reminds me of lining up at a theme park to go on a scary ride—once you get to those front gates, there's no turning back, it's your turn next. I am about to go on the scariest ride of my life. This makes Disney's 'Tower of Terror' look like a kiddie ride in a shopping mall.

The television on the wall is screening a morning news program, but I am so nervous I can't concentrate on anything the newsreader is saying.

In the chair beside me, James flips through the pages of a book that my Dad had given him, *Don't Sweat the Small Stuff... and It's All Small Stuff,* by Dr Richard Carlson. I start to read a bit of it over his shoulder.

One of the chapters in the book is titled: "Remember, One Hundred Years from Now, All New People." Oh my gosh, I get the giggles reading that profound statement. I begin laughing hysterically as I am struck with the sudden realisation of the impermanence of life. James looks at me like I am nuts.

SURGERY

In the midst of laughing at that one sentence, myself and my predicament, I come to a deep understanding of how accurate it is. The people who have gone before us—our relatives and ancestors—have all had their individual struggles, trials and tribulations. From poverty, wars, the Great Depression, illnesses, injuries, deaths, divorces and family dramas. But we, their descendants, don't worry about what they went through. We're not even thinking about it. It doesn't matter anymore. It's done. They're gone. One hundred years from now, no one will remember this moment. No one will care what I went through, how much I suffered or how stressful it was for me. No one will probably even know, in any great detail, what took place during my lifetime. My name will be just that: a name listed alongside a date of birth and date of death on a piece of paper (or, more likely, a family tree research program on the Internet).

I latch onto that chapter title like a drowning person holding a life preserver. This one sentence, in this small but insightful book, strikes me with incredible pertinence.

Everything passes with time. We only have this immediate moment. That is all. This one significant moment in time, in which to choose our thoughts about life. It's extraordinary that the right words at the right time can be like an anchor during a *dark night of the soul*. Words alone do not teach, but they can help guide you back to safety and re-establish your equilibrium.

My attention shifts back to the room and the people around me. A young woman in front of us appears exceedingly nervous and jittery. Clearly on edge, her legs bounce up and down as she peers apprehensively at every nurse who enters the room.

The personal boundaries that I would ordinarily have in place in this type of situation—talking to strangers in a hospital waiting room prior to major surgery—dissolve, and without thinking about it, I put my hand on her shoulder and say softly, "You look anxious, is there anything I can do for you?"

She turns to face me, and we begin talking. She tells me her two-year-old daughter had gone in for a tonsillectomy that morning. We chat about our families for a little while before she is called away by the nurse.

The woman thanks me for the conversation as she leaves to go and see her daughter. I feel wonderfully uplifted as our brief interaction distracted me from the uneasiness of my own wait.

I instantly realise that the secret to happiness in this *now* moment is really very simple: kindness to every living thing. The quickest way to get out of the doldrums and stop feeling sorry for yourself is to help another person in need. To put aside your own concerns and, instead, focus on serving others.

SURGERY

I suddenly feel a sense of love and joy around me as I realise I don't need to be scared. I need not fear. Nothing can *really* hurt me. I can see how all the hard times I have experienced have helped me to deal with adversity, propelling me to be *more* than I was before.

I am jolted from my state of contemplation as I hear my name being called. James and I follow the nurse into the tiny room. The nurse takes down my details and motions for me to hold out my wrist so she can attach a hospital ID band.

"It's time to go, Kim," the nurse says. James squeezes my hand tightly. He kisses me goodbye, and our eyes meet for one last moment while we silently convey a lifetime of love to one another.

The nurse hands me a gown and directs me to exit out a door at the back of the room, which I now realise is the exit door to get to surgery.

I step through the doorway into a corridor with change rooms off to one side. I find an empty cubicle and proceed to get undressed. Well, wouldn't you know it, the gown is a newfangled one, and I can't work out how to get it on! I simply can't tell the front from the back and I end up in knots and fits of giggles trying to fit into it. A kind nurse, hearing my struggle, comes to the rescue and finally helps me into the gown.

The nurse leads me to a large room filled with people

lying in hospital beds, waiting to go into surgery. She directs me to an empty bed.

As I climb onto the thin mattress, I notice the panicked expressions on the faces of the patients around me, and I suddenly feel anxious all over again. I try to breathe deeply and calm myself down. I pull the sheet up over my head and silently say goodbye to my breasts.

A memory flashes in my mind from when I was eleven years old. One night, after my shower, I locked myself in the bathroom, urging my breasts to grow. Then puberty hit, and it seems they sprang up overnight. My breasts became huge!

Since then they have always been a source of pleasure and pain. I welcomed the attention that men gave me because of them, but I was also perturbed by the jealousy, envy and competitiveness directed at me from other women.

When I gave birth to Nathaniel, my breasts really came into their own. Our son was born eight weeks prematurely. He was very tiny and sick. The doctors and nurses in the neonatal intensive care unit encouraged me to express colostrum, which they would feed him via a nasogastric tube. I began expressing immediately, a few hours after giving birth, one precious drop of *liquid gold* at a time. I only managed to get about one millilitre at first, but I persevered and managed to hand-express for the entire time I was in hospital.

The nurses froze my breast milk until Nathaniel learned

to suckle properly so it could be given to him by bottle. I was so proud that I was able to provide this nourishment for our premature son.

Nathaniel quickly grew, gained weight and thrived. He was allowed home from the hospital a full five weeks before the doctors had initially predicted.

When we were discharged from the hospital, a nurse asked my husband to bring a cooler bag and retrieve the unused frozen milk to take home. There were *fifty* bottles in the freezer! The nurses were impressed. My breasts were amazing milk machines!

Nathaniel took to breastfeeding like a duck to water, and I breastfed him for the next twelve months. *Finally! This is what they were made for!* When Nicholas arrived, I breastfed him for a similar period of time.

I always took such great care of my breasts. They have been an important part of my whole life. I am devastated that now I am losing them!

A wave of courage suddenly washes over me as I realise I'm not losing my breasts—I'm losing cancer! This operation is necessary for my survival. *I can do this!* I am not going to be in any way diminished as a person. I will still be whole, I will still be a woman. It's up to me, and me alone, to change my perspective on this situation and fully realise this with every fibre of my being.

As I am wheeled to the operating theatre, I make peace with myself, my breasts, and everything this experience of having cancer has to teach me. I've been strong before. I can be even stronger now.

I am tickled pink to see the anaesthetist is wearing a bandana adorned with characters from the animated sitcom *The Simpsons*. I have been a huge fan since I was a teenager, and our whole family has grown up watching the popular series. In fact, I would rather watch that hilarious cartoon family than the depressing nightly news.

Seeing these familiar cartoon characters on this woman's bandana brings a touch of light-heartedness to an otherwise stressful ordeal. I will never forget this moment. I get the feeling she is a guardian angel in disguise.

Breathe. Moment. Breathe. One by one, these moments make up my life.

SURGERY

"Experience is the teacher of all things."

— Julius Caesar

Recovery

I wake up to the overpowering odour of hospital disinfectant invading my nostrils. I slowly attempt to prise my dry, scratchy eyes open, squinting in an effort to sharpen my blurred vision.

Completely disoriented, I scrutinise the room around me. The walls are the colour of oatmeal, the floor a murky brown. A crisp white, linen sheet is pulled up under my armpits and tucked neatly at my sides.

How long have I been here?

I try to recall what happened before I went under the anaesthetic. I remember scooting over from the hospital gurney onto the surgery table...my surgeon's smiling eyes, warm and reassuring over the top of his surgical mask...

other staff milling about, methodically arranging medical instruments...someone told me to count backwards from ten, but I only got to nine before sinking into oblivion...

As realisation dawns, an excruciating pain suddenly obliterates every other sensation in my body. I breathe in short, ragged breaths—a futile attempt to minimise the pain.

My moans quickly summon the nurse to my bedside, and she injects something into my drip. The blinding agony gradually fades to a dull throb, ebbing and flowing like the tide.

Carefully lifting my gown, I'm startled to see two mounds where my breasts used to be. Long, plastic tubes have been inserted and stitched into place under my armpits. I can feel them curled under the skin around the top of my chest. It's the most sickening feeling.

Further down, the tubes attach to little plastic bottles by the sides of my body. They remind me of the hand grenade-shaped cordial drinks I occasionally had as a child. These bottles appear to collect the blood and fluid from the surgical site—it's so gross. I have a new respect for nurses. The stuff they deal with must make their toes curl.

I'm very uncomfortable, and it's difficult to change positions in the hospital bed. I move as cautiously as I can, but each movement catapults me into agony. I feel as though I have been tickled by 'Wolverine'.

The after-effects of surgery are tough. It's much more

painful and horrifying than I expected. I have never endured such a level of pain before. It alternates between burning and throbbing, easing off to aching, then back again to a white-hot stabbing. Childbirth now seems like a walk in the park compared to this. I will never complain about any pain, *ever* again.

Without warning, I begin to vomit everywhere. The nurse appears and calmly hands me a sickness bag and explains that I may be reacting to the painkillers. She steps out of the room to get some medication to help with the nausea and vomiting. Every time I retch, it pulls at the muscles around my chest.

Tomorrow's another day. I've got to start feeling better soon.

Friday, 5th September

Everything still hurts. I have been given two little hand-stitched satin pillows to protect the areas that have been operated on. They are shaped like small handbags with a strap at the top that I've placed over my shoulders. I can move the pillow part to the side or across my chest, depending on where I need support. These pillows have been lovingly made by volunteers who evidently saw a need for mastectomy patients. How very kind of them to do this, not to mention extremely practical. These little pillows have already become my constant companions—total security blanket status!

A surprise visitor walks into my room holding a huge bunch of flowers. It's the woman I met in the waiting room before my surgery. I can hear the relief in her voice as she tells me her daughter will be going home today. She hands me the flowers and expresses her gratitude for our chat yesterday, explaining how it helped calm her nerves. I am in awe that she has taken the time to come and see me to show her appreciation. How kind and selfless—and entirely unexpected.

We say our goodbyes, and as she leaves the room, I reflect on this extraordinary exchange. We were complete strangers who connected on a deep level and mutually helped each other when we were both feeling vulnerable. How easy it would have been to ignore each other's plight and focus on our own worries. By putting aside our own concerns and reaching out, we helped ease each other's pain, and by doing so, we touched each other's lives.

The busy lifestyle that we all seem to lead leaves little time for gratitude. We might think we are alone, but really, we are all connected—humans living together on the same planet, just trying to do the best we can.

Instead of being selfish, always focusing on ourselves, perhaps we should begin to see what we can do to inspire others to rise in the face of adversity. Impossible challenges can be overcome with the help of others.

Sunday, 7th September

I lay staring at the ceiling, wondering what my family is doing at home. I miss them all so much, but I realise it is easier to rest and recover here in the hospital without my rambunctious boys running around.

The surgical ward ran out of beds last night, so I had to change rooms. I'm now in the children's ward, but they will need this room for kids coming in for surgery tomorrow, so it looks like I will have to be moved again.

The nurse enters the room and begins refilling my water glass.

"So, you're going home tomorrow?" she asks chirpily.

I stare blankly at her, trying to form a response. I think to myself, *Have you seen me, lady? Do I look I'm ready to go home and look after two kids and a household again?*

Although she may be overly optimistic about how quickly I am improving, I don't feel any better. I am still sore and traumatised by the operation, and I only managed to get a couple of hours of broken sleep last night. Surely I'll need a few more days of recuperation before I am sent home?

I am able to use the toilet by myself, but I still need help to shower, as I'm not allowed to raise my arms above my head. I have to give the breast implants the best possible chance to heal in place.

James washed me for the first time yesterday. Poor guy, it took him an hour! He had the shakes by the time he finished. My hair was challenging to wash because it was all matted with vomit. Eww, disgusting.

My long hair is going to be difficult to manage when I go home. Thankfully Nicole, my sister-in-law, popped in yesterday afternoon and plaited my hair. That will save me from having to worry about it for the next week or so.

The hardest part about getting undressed is seeing myself in the mirror. My reflection stares dully back at me, face pale and waxy, with eyes like limpid pools in shadow. There are two swollen lumps on my chest, with crisscrossed lines of blood-soaked bandages. It is a pretty gruesome sight. I can't help but feel sorry for myself.

I'm gradually getting my appetite back, but it's somewhat challenging to manoeuvre myself to eat. James has been trying to make it in for lunch time and dinner so he can help me, but annoyingly, I've missed breakfast a couple of times because the attendant left my meal on the other side of the room and I couldn't reach it.

My sleep patterns have been sporadic, and I wake frequently. I have been having the most intense and frightening dreams. In these terrifying nightmares, I am lost in a deserted, post-apocalyptic city, trying in vain to find my way home.

It's bizarre how fears can manifest themselves in dreams. I've woken up drenched in sweat a number of times, only to realise that I am actually living a *real* nightmare at the moment. I can only hope that things will begin to look and feel a bit more positive soon.

I have a lot of time to think while lying in the hospital bed. I keep reliving the diagnosis, over and over again. Each time my mind runs ahead to various pessimistic scenarios and possible future outcomes.

It takes a lot of effort to try and remain focused and keep my thoughts positive—I would love a distraction from my ruminating. I find myself spending a lot of time counting down the minutes until the next visitor appears.

Nicholas is still recovering from pneumonia and I feel guilty that I have not been there to comfort him during his illness, as a mother usually does.

James has had to take on the duties of both parents and has been taking great care of Nicholas, ensuring he keeps his fluids up and takes his medicine. Dad has also been looking after the boys while James is with me at the hospital. These remarkable men in my life make a great team.

Monday, 8th September

Home at last! I am so glad to be back in familiar surroundings. As I enter the house, the comforting floral aroma of freshly washed clothes gives me relief from the antiseptic smell of the hospital. The boys greet me enthusiastically and I've never felt so loved.

I'll be spending the next few weeks inactive—either in bed sleeping or on the lounge watching television or reading. I am unaccustomed to sitting or lying around all day, and I know I'm going to feel useless. It will be a challenge to rest and do nothing.

My world has become very small.

Wednesday, 10th September

James has been an absolute darling. He's really stepped up to the plate since I came home from hospital. He continually checks on me to make sure I'm comfortable.

The boys have also been fantastic. They have been so gentle. I'm seeing a whole other side of them, and it's vastly different from the rough-and-tumble boys they usually are.

The surgery site is still painful, and I am exhausted, both physically and emotionally. I still need James to help with showering. It's tiring on us both to get in the shower without bumping any sore parts, as well as trying to manage the drains and bottles that are still attached to my body.

I have an appointment to see my surgeon at his office tomorrow to find out whether the surgery was successful. I'll also get to meet my oncologist for the first time, and I'm anxious to see what my next steps will be.

Thursday, 11th September

As I perch nervously at the edge of the chair opposite my surgeon's desk, I feel my anxiety rise and begin to take hold.

"Good news," the surgeon smiles at me. I breathe an enormous sigh of relief. The surgery was successful, and all of the lymph nodes were clear. Thank God! The surgeon explains the pathology results indicated there were three tumours. I am shocked. Clearly, I made the right decision to have a mastectomy.

The oncologist joins us in the surgeon's office and greets me warmly. He is lovely, like a kindly uncle. I feel safe and comfortable in his presence. He advises that the next step is chemotherapy, which will be administered intravenously at the oncology outpatients clinic once a week, for three months.

Each treatment will last approximately two or three hours. Even though the cancer was not found in the lymph nodes, the chemotherapy will kill and mop up any stray cancer cells that may have escaped. The oncologist explains that, following chemotherapy, I will be injected with a new 'wonder drug' every three weeks for 12 months. *I wonder what it does?* I think to myself. I will also have to take medication for the next ten years as a deterrent for hormone receptor-positive breast cancer. Both doctors reassure me I've had a good result.

The oncologist mentions I will lose my hair, but I shouldn't suffer from too much nausea as the chemotherapy I will be having has fewer side effects than other types.

I think I will donate my long, brunette locks to a charity that makes wigs for people who have lost theirs. Maybe I can get a rockin' short haircut!

Saturday, 20th September

The wounds appear to be healing well. I'm still bandaged up, but I can see the discharge from the drains is slowing down, day by day.

I can't wait to get these drains out. They are uncomfortable, and it's annoying to carry them around all the time. The hospital gave me a little cotton bag to put over my shoulder to carry the bottles in. It has been lovingly sewn by a volunteer who obviously experienced what a nuisance these drains are.

Each day I have to empty the two containers of blood and fluid, check for signs of infection and measure the output, writing the results on a chart. I dry-retch every time I have to do it. I'm grateful James can help me with the practicalities of this. He's an absolute saint, and I realise how fortunate I am to have a husband like him.

I'm so tired, yet I can't sleep! I'm wired from the seemingly constant stream of visitors who have called in to see me. People seem to be coming out of the woodwork! I've caught up with friends whom I had lost touch with over the past few years.

It's really lovely that people want to see me, and I'm grateful for the conversation, but I wonder: do they think I'm dying or something? I appreciate the gesture, but having so many visitors right now is tiring. I am expending a lot of my energy interacting with and entertaining each visitor. When I see their sad and pitying faces, I feel like I need to say uplifting, positive things to try and cheer them up. It's terribly exhausting.

I'm going to have to limit visitors once I start the chemotherapy on Monday. I know people mean well, but I'm so tired and cranky from lack of sleep. My friend, Wendy, jokingly told me to put a sign on my front door:

Morning visitors welcome from 10:00 a.m. to 11:30 a.m. Children to be left in the car or tied to the front tree. The patient needs to rest from 11:30 a.m. to 3:00 p.m. Afternoon visiting hours from 3:00 p.m. to 4:00 p.m.

I don't want to risk alienating my friends and people who care deeply about me, but I'm seriously considering putting up the sign!

Sunday, 21st September

Mentally preparing myself for chemotherapy is tough. Having watched Mum when she went through her treatment, I know this is not going to be easy. She was nauseous all the time and found it extremely taxing. Her white blood cell count dropped to extremely low levels and she became neutropenic, which made her more susceptible to infection. Mum had to be admitted to hospital and put on a drip a couple of times. I'm scared. I wish Mum were still here to help me get through this.

I am starting to think about what it will be like losing my crowning glory—my extremely long, dark brown hair. How long until it starts to fall out? I've heard that it can happen pretty quickly, within a couple of days once chemotherapy begins.

How will it make me feel? What will people think when they see me? When I'm out, say, at the shopping centre, will I be the subject of the 'sympathetic smile'?

How will my hair grow back? I hope it grows back! What if the hair cells are permanently damaged, and I'm bald for the rest of my life? Will it grow back a different colour? I've heard that chemotherapy sometimes stimulates the cells to produce colour again, and patients have fewer greys when their hair does grow back. Maybe I will dye my hair blonde. I have always wondered if blondes do have more fun. Then there is apparently 'chemo curls' to look forward to. It would be strange to have curls after having dead-straight hair all my life.

I've decided I'll get my hair cut short. Then, when it starts to fall out, I will get it shaved. I don't want to look like 'Beetlejuice', with bald patches scattered amongst clumps of thinning hair.

My oncologist told me it will start to fall out in week eight of chemotherapy. I guess I'll see. Apparently, the most common question oncologists are asked when they tell people they have cancer isn't, "Will I die?" but, "Will my hair fall out?"

We humans are so vain.

"One does not become enlightened by imagining figures of light, but by making the darkness conscious."

— Carl Jung

Chemotherapy

Monday, 22nd September

My brother-in-law and his wife arrive to collect our sons for a day out at the playground. I wave goodbye and take a deep breath as they drive off down the street. A new routine begins today: it's my first day of chemotherapy.

I have twelve weeks of treatment ahead of me, and it feels daunting. It seems like a long time until I will be done and I am already dreading this part of my life. I hope this time passes quickly.

I am no stranger to needles. I have been receiving treatment for a mild form of Osteogenesis Imperfecta, or 'brittle bone syndrome', diagnosed after I fractured my shoulder eight years ago. The treatment for this involves having an intravenous bisphosphonate drug, injected every month, to prevent the loss of bone density.

Arriving at the hospital, we are lucky enough to find a parking spot close to the entrance. Hopefully, this is a good omen for the day.

As we enter the clinic, I notice the sign says 'Chemotherapy Suite'. It almost sounds like a fancy hotel!

Once inside I am struck by how new and spotlessly clean everything is. Even the armchair recliners look luxurious and comfortable. They are lined up in two rows facing each other, with an equipment station in the middle of the room.

I notice a row of framed lightboxes in the ceiling with pictures of blue sky and wispy, white clouds on them. It is like looking through a skylight to a vivid sky above. Of course, in reality, the next level of the hospital is above us, but what a lovely touch for the patients.

The nurses smile brightly as they move serenely around the room, tending to their patients. A nurse approaches and politely asks James to wait outside while I am shown to an armchair at the end of one of the rows. The nurse is a sturdy, no-nonsense woman with a friendly smile and the relaxed aura of someone who's seen it all before. She seems to radiate a calming presence with her soothing voice and compassionate persona. I warm to her immediately, and I feel as though

CHEMOTHERAPY

I can instantly trust her. She explains what will happen today and what my routine will be for the next few months.

The nurse inserts a cannula into the top of my left wrist, explaining that because the lymph nodes were removed on my right side, where the cancer had been, I would need to use my left arm for chemotherapy or any other needles in future. Her technique is gentle and efficient, and the needle only stings a tiny bit. Once I am set up on the drip, she calls James in and shows him to the chair next to mine.

The nurse flushes the drip with a bag of saline solution, before administering an antihistamine and a steroid medication which, she explains, is to help minimise any adverse reaction to the chemotherapy. Finally, she infuses the chemotherapy drug into the drip. And now we wait.

I notice a small kitchenette in the corner of the room. On the bench rests a tray with jugs of juice and water. Beside it is a hot water urn and sachets of tea and coffee. James hops up to check it out and is excited to discover the fridge is full of little triangle sandwiches, packets of cheese slices and biscuits, tubs of flavoured yoghurt, and ice blocks in the freezer. He returns with two cups of tea and some sandwiches.

I feel quite relaxed, sipping my tea and sinking gently back into the plush recliner. I haven't had any unpleasant effects so far, except for a strong metallic taste in my mouth.

Apart from the needles, and the fact that I am hooked

up for cancer treatment, this experience is not as bad as I thought it would be. If you didn't think too deeply about it, and if you were the sort of person who could easily visualise yourself somewhere else while this horrendous thing was going on, you would probably find it quite bearable.

I look at the other patients around us. Most of them have gone bald already. Some are wearing scarves or woollen beanies on their heads. I try to strike up a conversation with a couple of people nearby, but they don't seem very receptive to talking, perhaps even a little bit grouchy too, but I smile at them anyway. Maybe they are feeling unwell or depressed, I'm not sure. I don't feel sick at all, thank goodness.

A representative from the company who makes the drip lines observes the goings-on in the room, spending quite a bit of time talking to us and explaining how the drips work. It is all rather interesting.

A small television, suspended from the roof, is showing *The Ellen DeGeneres Show*. She must be the funniest woman on Earth. Being able to have a good, hearty laugh is great. It takes my mind off the reason why I am here. The nurses watch us, amused, as James and I giggle at the antics on screen. Coincidentally, the episode showing is about celebrating women who have had breast cancer. As the program concludes, Ellen asks viewers to send in their stories about their experience. The thought crosses my mind that I should take a photo of myself, having chemotherapy while watching her show and email it in.

Arriving home after a long three-and-a-half hours at the clinic, I feel tired and have the beginnings of a headache. The boys burst into the house after a fun day of playing with their cousins, and my sister-in-law surprises us with a delicious, home-cooked dinner. This is, hands down, the world's best gift when you are ill. It certainly takes the pressure off having to think about what to cook for dinner. My lovely neighbour also called in with a lasagne, peppermint slice and chocolate chip cookies for the boys.

Other gifts that have been delivered have been absolutely delightful. I will never forget the kindness our friends and family have shown us in sharing their time and energy. Beautiful flowers, magazines and books, soaps and hand creams—even a washing basket full of practical items. My heart is full of love for these kind, considerate and thoughtful people who have helped us in our time of need.

Saturday, 27th September

I've woken up with an angry red rash on my face and chest, and I feel boiling hot all over. The nurse had warned me that an allergic reaction like this could develop.

The steroids I was given during chemotherapy made me

very manic and high for the first few days, and I had trouble sleeping. But last night I went to bed at 6:30 p.m. and slept, undisturbed, until 7:30 a.m. this morning. James said he kept checking on me all night. I think he was worried I had died in my sleep.

Will the after-effects of chemotherapy be like this every time? I am starting to feel a little down and slightly depressed.

As I lay on the lounge, writing in my journal, I have an epiphany—a remarkable realisation that I just have to play the hand that life has dealt me. When I begin to feel sorry for myself, perhaps I need to recognise that this is the way life is right now. Some things can't be changed. I have to take it and run with it. I need to make an effort to find the positives, however slim, and make the best of my situation. Acceptance of every circumstance in my life is the key to peace of mind. As James always says, "It is what it is." Yes, I've lost my breasts, but I'll never have to have another mammogram ever again. And I don't have to wear a bra anymore. See? Positives!

I've consciously decided to change my perspective and focus on the needs of others, rather than my own. I will stop the car and say hello to a friend instead of rushing past. I'll take a minute out of my day to send an uplifting message to someone going through a challenging time. I will make a quick phone call to a friend who might be feeling lonely. Or perhaps drop off a meal to a neighbour who is doing it a little tough at the moment. You never know the effect a simple act of kindness could have. Maybe spreading joy and making someone else's day a little brighter will make me happy too?

Monday, 6th October

There is no chemotherapy today, due to the public holiday. My treatment is delayed until tomorrow. I am glad because I couldn't face going to the hospital today. My hair has started to fall out, and my gums bleed when I brush my teeth. Minor issues, in the whole scheme of things, but still a little annoying and cause for some concern.

Thankfully, we've been invited to a barbecue lunch by our dear friends, the Hazells. It will be a refreshing change as I haven't been anywhere, apart from the hospital, for the past few weeks.

Arriving at their stunning home by the seaside, our cherished friends welcome us affectionately and the children run off to play in the backyard. As the conversation flows, I begin to forget about my troubles. The great thing about old friends is that you don't have to put on airs and graces or pretend to be anyone other than yourself.

After an enjoyable lunch, I become so relaxed that I have a little nap in the comfy daybed on the back porch. I feel renewed by the love and support I have received today, and I am ready to face another day of gruelling treatment tomorrow.

Wednesday, 8th October

I've woken up with another angry, red rash all over, this time from neck to knee. It looks like I have a severe case of chicken pox. I desperately phone the nurse for advice. Apparently, it's a drug rash, caused by my body trying to get the chemotherapy drug out of my system.

My hair is also now falling out in clumps. It's awfully distressing. My bed looks like a shaggy dog has rolled in it. The bathroom floor is covered with long, dark strands of hair. Anyone would think a yeti had a shave in there. I'm *freaking* out! My head feels extremely sore, and I have an achy, throbbing feeling on my scalp like I've had my hair in a high, tight ponytail.

It's bizarre to think that the doctors are administering a medicine so poisonous that it's giving me this awful rash and making my hair fall out!

James is back at work today. It's good for him to get out of the house and have some normality again, but I miss him.

I am visited by two of my cherished girlfriends who are part of a close group of friends I've had since primary school. These women are like sisters to me. They are the most beautiful, gentle souls, each possessing their own unique gifts and talents, and I treasure our friendship.

As busy mums, we don't get to catch up very often, but we all go away together on a girls' getaway each year, which is coming up this weekend. We have so much fun together, hardly drawing breath for the whole weekend, and talking nonstop well into the night. These women know my family history and all my stories, and I can always rely on them to have my back.

The girls present me with a beautiful, handmade quilt that they have all created together. The quilt is incredible! What a grand gesture—a totally unexpected and delightful surprise. I am touched that they've all had a hand in it. They each separately picked out some meaningful patterned fabric, representing things I like, such as dragonflies and the colour pink. It is indeed made with love.

They share with me the funny stories of dragging their kids unwillingly to the haberdashery store and how they managed to collaborate on this project while keeping it secret.

I am so lucky and grateful to have these wonderful women as my lifelong friends. They are my spiritual sisters—my *sisters of light*. I'm taking the quilt with me to chemotherapy next time I go—I can't wait to show the nurses.

When Mum was sick, her friends got together to sew her a beautiful quilt as well. How *serendipitous* that my friends, without knowing about this, did the exact same thing for me. I can't help but feel that, somehow, Mum was able to influence their hearts from Heaven.

Saturday, 11th October

It's wonderful to finally be in the Hunter Valley, on my annual trip away with my lovely girlfriends. We are staying in a cute bungalow, overlooking an olive-green dam and surrounded by huge gum trees and an abundance of native birdlife.

I didn't sleep very soundly last night, despite the serenity, but I am enjoying our relaxing time together, sharing beautiful meals and visiting markets and quaint, little country stores.

While enjoying breakfast at a café, I am suddenly overcome with an intense, anxious feeling in the pit of my stomach, which rises up so fiercely it brings me to tears.

My friends' valiant attempts to console me are futile, as my brain unpredictably begins to spew out worrisome thoughts. It's like my mind is creating frightening visions of the future with terrifying potential outcomes.

Even though I know that these thoughts have no logical basis, I seem to have no control over them. I begin to imagine the doctors have lied to me and that I am going to die. It feels like my mind has been taken over by some malicious entity.

As my friends watch helplessly, I hysterically phone James in the hope that the sound of his voice will help calm me down. Through streaming tears, I desperately look around the table at my friends, who all appear terribly worried about my state of mind. It upsets me to think I have ruined the weekend for them.

Home seems like the only place I can feel safe and secure right now, and I am anxious to return.

Tuesday, 14th October

I meet with my oncologist for a progress report and share with him how I am coping with the chemotherapy treatment.

I describe a sensation I've been suffering from, which feels like a 'frozen' shoulder. He discovers I have something called Axillary Web Syndrome, or 'cording', a rare side-effect caused by the removal of my lymph nodes. I have a thick 'rope' of protruding muscle extending from my armpit all the way down the underside of my arm, nearly to my wrist. It feels extremely tight and sore, and I can barely raise my arm.

After the appointment, the oncologist sends me next door to the Occupational Therapist, who massages my arm to loosen the taut muscles. She explains that the cording is an inflammation of the lymph channel, but that I shouldn't worry too much as it will settle itself in time. It feels like another hurdle to overcome in a seemingly endless list of annoying side-effects.

I've noticed that my previously 20/20 vision has become distorted and I can't read signs in the distance like I could before starting treatment. I wonder if the chemotherapy has damaged my eyesight?

I've lost my appetite, and I'm still not sleeping well either. I'm suffering from intense hot flushes due to the onset of menopause, and I feel exhausted most of the time. When I do manage to sleep, I have terrifying nightmares. Thankfully, for the moment, I haven't had any more anxiety attacks. That whole experience at the café has left a bad taste in my mouth, and it has made me scared and uncomfortable.

I had my fourth chemotherapy treatment yesterday. Eight more rounds to go. I feel pretty awful today—nauseous, fatigued and my hair continues to fall out at a rapid rate. I was hoping to keep as much of it as I could until after our family reunion next weekend because I don't want to freak out all the little kids.

I've had so many differing opinions about when I will lose all my hair. Some have said it may not fall out completely, but thin out instead. I wonder if losing my hair will be cathartic? Like pressing the reset button on life. A new beginning. Maybe it's time for a new hairstyle? *And a new me?*

I phone my friend Nicole, a hairdresser, who agrees to come right over with her clippers. It's now or never...

Monday, 20th October

Shaving my head last week was a horrible and confronting experience, but I'm trying to look on the bright side. At least I felt immediate relief from the burning ache on my scalp.

The doctor has given me the all-clear to start driving, so I've decided I'm going shopping tomorrow. Nicholas' tenth birthday is coming up next month, and I'm excited to be able to go out to buy him a present.

Friends have called in a few nights this week to bring dinner for us. How incredibly kind of them. Managing to cook dinner for us, in the midst of looking after their own families is a magnificent gesture. These friends truly embody humanity at its finest. I will be forever grateful for their kind-heartedness and compassion.

Sunday, 26th October

The day of our annual family reunion is finally here. We all absolutely love getting together but, because we live in different regions, we found it hard to see each other regularly, and it got to the point where we were only meeting up for weddings or funerals. So, a few years ago, we began a yearly tradition, where all the families could meet at a centrally-located park, for a day of sharing food, fun and generally feeling the love and sense of family connection.

I think it's absolutely fantastic for all of us, especially the younger kids, to gain a sense of connection to the extended family. Everyone in our family is big-hearted, kind, affectionate and accepting. Being part of our family means you are loved, no matter what.

My relatives are shocked to see my bald head, but I am revelling in the funny side of it. Dad recently shaved his head in solidarity, and we take some hilarious photos of our bald heads together.

Today is the most fun I've had in ages. It is great to feel like part of something bigger than myself. I feel loved, connected and supported. My family is the best!

Monday, 27th October

My veins are not cooperating at chemotherapy today. Three veins collapsed when the nurse tried to insert the cannula.

Chemotherapy has thrown me right smack-bang into the middle of menopause, and I am having hot flushes all the time. My oncologist has assured me this is normal, but it sure doesn't *feel* normal to me. As 'Morticia Addams' said,

CHEMOTHERAPY

"Normal is an illusion. What is normal for the spider, is chaos for the fly."

It has taken an enormous amount of energy to make it this far in my healing process, so I've been trying to listen to my body and not overdo it, resting whenever I can. Sure, the chores may not get done, but they can wait until later. Who cares if we have a messy house? No one! I want to make sure my boys have a well-rested mum, who's not too tired to spend time with them.

The breast care nurse visits after chemotherapy and takes me to a private examination room to remove my dressings and bandages. It takes some effort—those things are stuck fast! Some adhesive remover fluid finally does the trick to get the sticky residue off my skin, revealing the fresh pink scars underneath. I'm pleased to see the great job my body has done in healing the wounds.

Eager to inspect my chest more closely, I timidly take a few steps towards the mirror above the sink, bracing myself as I study my reflection.

The person peering back at me looks vastly different from what I am used to. I study the *new* me for a few moments, taking it all in, while I mentally come to terms with this new form.

The skin on my chest is stretched tightly over the implants, and appears slightly swollen and almost translucent. I notice, with a wry sense of amusement, that the faded stretch marks that used to be at the top of my breasts—badges of honour from my breastfeeding days—are now stretched along the sides and beneath my new 'breasts'. The thought crosses my mind that I resemble a mannequin pieced together from spare parts.

I look thinner than I was before the surgery. My cheeks are gaunt and hollowed, and there are dark smudges underneath my eyes. But my appearance takes a back seat as I realise how lucky I am to finally have the cancer out of my body. Now the healing of body and mind begins.

Friday, 14th November

The shock and trauma of the surgery is now starting to fade and I feel like I'm entering into 'warrior woman' phase. I've experienced some rough patches recently, but a sense of inner strength is beginning to rise and I am smart enough to realise what doesn't kill me makes me stronger than ever.

I'm starting to realise that I've *got* this. I can do it! I have surpassed my own expectations of coping with the after-effects of surgery, the chemotherapy and all the associated unpleasant side-effects. Knowing that makes me feel empowered and more in control of my life.

I appreciate what a gift I have been given—this opportunity to survive—and I'm not wasting any more time feeling sad or anxious or depressed. I've done enough of that for one lifetime. I'm embracing happiness and joy whenever I can.

Every morning, when I wake up, I say to myself, "I am in perfect health," and I picture myself brimming with positive well-being.

Something I've found that's been helping me a lot is finding inspirational quotes or words, either in books or on television or social media. I've started writing down a few passages here and there that resonate with me so I can reread them later. I've printed a dozen or so of my favourite quotes on big sheets of paper and sticky-taped them up on my kitchen wall. Each morning when I wake up feeling a little low, I read one of the quotes, and it helps me get hold of my worries and gives me something to focus on.

The kids were watching an old *Loony Tunes* cartoon on television. In one scene 'Bugs Bunny' goes to the doctor and is mistakenly diagnosed with a grave illness. When the doctor finally realises his mistake, he phones Bugs to give him the good news. The doctor says, "You're in perfect health! Go out, enjoy your life. Live a little." What sound advice!

Our oldest and dearest friends, the Newell family, have started calling around and bringing dinner over on Friday nights. It's become the highlight of my week. Being able to talk and laugh with our friends over a delicious home-cooked meal is immeasurably blissful. With all the doctor's appointments and waiting rooms that have taken over my world lately, it's nice to have some semblance of a normal social life and feel like a human being again, instead of just a patient.

Wednesday, 3rd December

I've booked myself in for a Look Good Feel Better workshop,² a cancer initiative that helps patients learn how to manage the appearance-related side effects of cancer treatment. The brochure explains: *"The aim is to help them feel empowered and ready to face their cancer diagnosis with confidence."*

I am nervous turning up alone—I didn't think beforehand to arrange for a friend to come with me.

Arriving at the centre, I am enthusiastically welcomed by the organisers and immediately made to feel right at home. Alongside other cancer patients, I take part in a workshop with beauticians and makeup artists, who have volunteered their time to educate us on skin care during chemotherapy, how to apply makeup to minimise chemotherapy effects and how to style a scarf or select a wig. I receive a Confidence Kit—a bag full of skincare and makeup products donated by the cosmetic industry.

For a few, short hours, I feel like a woman again. What a

precious experience. I am so thankful for the opportunity to attend, and I am grateful to these volunteers for giving their time and expertise.

This experience is so much more than just makeup and wigs. It is a real boost to my self-esteem.

Sunday, 14th December

Christmas is fast approaching, so James and I take Nathaniel and Nicholas to the shopping centre to have their photo taken with Santa. It's a sweltering, hot Summer's day so I tie a cotton scarf over my bald head. The boys eagerly chat to Santa about what they want for Christmas, while I stand off to the side taking delight in seeing my children's happiness and enjoying the magic of Christmas.

After the boys finish having their photo taken, Santa catches my eye and motions for me to come forward. With smiling eyes he tells me how wonderful my boys are and how impressed he was by their polite manners, remarking on the great job I have done in raising them. I feel tears spring to my eyes as my heart bursts with pride. How considerate of this gentleman to go out of his way to make such lovely comments about my boys. All the challenges and hardships I have faced seem to melt away with the warmth of his words.

Thursday, 25th December

Christmas Day dawns bright and sunny. The boys tear around the house, shrieking in delight as they open their presents.

I finished chemotherapy a little over a week ago. I now have a short break before continuing on a different medication infusion. How different this Christmas is compared to those in the past. Usually, our whole family would get together at our house for a huge feast. By contrast, today we spend the quietest Christmas Day ever with Dad and my brother, David.

We enjoy a modest lunch of cold meat, salad and trifle. I can't help but reflect on how wonderful it is to simply be alive at this time. It dawns on me that Christmas has now taken on a whole new meaning, and with it, a deeper appreciation of the preciousness of all life.

Monday, 29th December

I've been desperate for a change of scenery but, since we haven't had a lot of income coming in over the past few months, taking a holiday is out of the question. Usually, the time you most need a holiday is when you can least afford it. Out of the blue, a relative has generously offered us the chance to stay at their on-site caravan near the beach for a couple of days between Christmas and New Year.

After driving for hours in the hot car, we arrive at a picturesque beach, nestled amongst the most beautiful surrounds. I am going to make the most of this. We immediately change into our swimsuits and race down the hill towards the pristine white sand. I can taste the saltiness in the air, and I can't wait to feel the cool water against my skin.

I take my hat off, revealing my shiny, bald head and I can't help but notice the astonished glances from the other beach-goers. It's a familiar feeling of alienation—one that I'm still getting used to. When I'm out in public, especially if I only wear a headscarf to cover my baldness, some people appear to be unusually shocked by the sight of me, virtually jumping out of my way. Do they think I have a contagious illness? Are they worried about *catching* cancer from me? As if I didn't feel alien enough!

Although I have lost most of the hair on my head and body, I have managed to retain a single row of hairs on my eyebrows. However, after leaving the surf and going back to the caravan to change, I catch myself in the mirror and discover, to my horror, those sparse eyebrows—the last thing that made me look human—have fallen out in the water. I am suddenly inconsolable and begin sobbing loudly.

"The surf took my eyebrows!" I wail. The boys and James look at each other for a moment, the corners of their eyes crinkling in amusement, before they all burst into hysterical laughter. Soon the tears are streaming down their faces as they try to catch their breath. Their laughter is contagious, and before long, I find myself giggling as well. My family sure is great to have around when I've been taking myself a little too seriously.

We settle in for the night and watch a funny movie from the nineties, *Coneheads,* starring Dan Aykroyd as the patriarch of an alien family. What I find wonderful about this movie is that the family are all completely bald, with comical, cone-shaped heads, yet they are completely accepted by society as they go about their business, living their lives normally. No one seems to think any less of them or be fazed by their bizarre-looking heads, and the wife and daughter are still considered beautiful, attractive and feminine.

Beauty is indeed only skin-deep. How I look on the outside does not define the person that I am. True beauty is found on the inside.

Monday, 26th January

It is nearly a whole month into the new year. Happy New Year. *Happy new me.*

It's only been a few weeks since I finished chemotherapy, and amazingly my hair has already started growing back—

CHEMOTHERAPY

I have a light layer of fine fuzz on my scalp—which is pleasantly surprising. I can't wait to see if it grows back differently. I'm so excited!

Although I still have ten months of medical infusions and hospital visits ahead of me, I feel like I'm on the home stretch. However, at the same time, my mental state has gone downhill with fretfulness and worry.

Weirdly, it was comforting being around the nurses and doctors every week. Now I feel like I'm left to my own devices. I should be happy to have finished with the chemotherapy so I can begin to get my normal life back, but all the positivity seems to have been sucked out of me.

Any and every pain I sense, anywhere in my body, causes me to think it's cancer. If I have a pain in my big toe, I immediately think, *It's toe cancer!* I know it's silly, and I'm not sure if other patients feel like this, post-treatment, but I just can't seem to help jumping to this irrational conclusion.

I've noticed I quickly become frustrated when people say to me, "You're fine now! The cancer is gone," but I'm having trouble moving forward with my life. It's like I'm stuck in wet cement, trapped and unable to focus on the bright future in front of me.

I am beginning to sense that I'm in for a wild emotional ride ahead.

"Hope perches in the soul. How it's not the denial of painful wounds, but the full awareness of those wounds, including the ways they could be healed."

— T. A. Barron, *The Wisdom Of Merlin*

Anxiety

Monday, 23rd February

If you haven't experienced anxiety, it's impossible to understand. Apart from the couple of panic attacks I've had since my diagnosis, I have never suffered from anxiety before.

Sure, I've had butterflies in my tummy, but this was usually accompanied by a feeling of nervous excitement and anticipation that something wonderful was about to happen. I once viewed people who suffered from anxiety as weak-minded. I would think to myself, *How hard can it be? Just get over it!*

My mother and grandmother both suffered from what they referred to as 'panic attacks'. Both had days where these panic attacks left them unable to leave the house. While I had sympathy for them, I did not have *empathy*. I would try to cajole them into cheering up—I didn't know how else to help them. I couldn't understand what they were going through or grasp how crippling their anxiety was. Until now.

It is alarming the way vile, negative and destructive thoughts have started to infiltrate my thinking. All throughout my surgery and chemotherapy, I was generally strong and confident. I was scared, sure, but I always maintained a hopeful feeling that things would get better.

Now, however, the minute I wake up my heart starts to beat a million miles a minute. I can't breathe, and it feels as though my chest is going to cave in. It is an unnerving and debilitating experience. What is happening to me? Is this a sign of an impending heart attack?

When I find myself experiencing anxiety, whether it's just anxious thinking or a full-blown panic attack, it is incredibly hard—in fact almost impossible—to get myself out of that dark place. It's like trying to find my way out of a labyrinth with a blindfold on. I literally don't know where to start. Eventually, everything unravels, and my anxiety gets out-of-control. Everything seems futile and hopeless. Once these negative thoughts take hold, it is too late to stop them.

I'm not sure what is going on. Maybe it's the medication

or menopause, but I have never felt things more intensely than right now.

Never in my life have I cried as much as in the past few weeks. Anything can set me off. A soppy television show, an emotional advertisement, something someone—especially my husband—said or did, or even my interpretation of it, now has me sobbing uncontrollably. It's like being pregnant again!

I've never been someone who publicly displayed their feelings, but now it's like I have been cracked wide open and emotions are pouring out of me. Strangers smiling at me in the supermarket can bring me to tears. Hearing a story about someone who's gone through a hard time, especially if it is related to cancer, leaves me inconsolable. In a single day, I can go through every human emotion, from joy and love, and feeling on top of the world, to fearfulness, anxiety and jealousy. It's exhausting and draining. This surely can't be normal. Am I psychotic?

I worry much more than usual about all kinds of calamities befalling me. I fear that James no longer fancies me and that he might leave. I imagine him quickly remarrying another woman, completely forgetting all about me and the tough times I have brought him. I fret that the doctors have made an error in my diagnosis and I worry about how my kids will cope if I die.

My mind goes immediately to the darkest place it can find, and I am suffocating under the weight of every painful thought.

As each new scenario becomes more ludicrous, I begin to think I am losing my sanity. I know, on some level, that these situations in my head are absurd, but it is as though my mind has completely taken over, running the show of who I actually am. I have started looking at every situation and experience in my life through a new filter: *cancer*.

I can no longer watch television, listen to the radio, or talk to people, as I feel I am being constantly bombarded with stories about people with cancer, or affected by some other tragic event or terrible misfortune.

If, in the middle of a conversation, someone starts to tell me a sad story, I become devastated beyond belief. I have to firmly tell them to stop and only continue with their story if it is a positive one with a happy ending, otherwise I can't stop thinking about what they have said for days. I feel helpless and powerless. People must think I am strange.

I have become reclusive, which is very out of character for me. I was always a happy, upbeat person, but now I can't show this depressed, anxious face to the world. I have sequestered myself away in the safe confinement of my home, terrified and unable to venture out each day.

I feel ashamed and scared that people will think of me

as a burden or a disappointment. They might not want to be around me. My friends and family are so used to always seeing my positive side, they may judge me as a failure if they only see the worst of me.

When I am forced to leave the house, I put on a façade of strength and lightness, but I'm unable to keep it up for long. I am vaguely aware, on some level, that those who love me are terribly worried about this change in my personality, but I can't bring myself to talk about my troubles with them.

I've lost my appetite, and I can't even eat a full-sized meal anymore. I know that I have to eat to keep my strength up, but mealtime has become a painful and bleak event. Every mouthful tastes bland, like shredded cardboard. The food turns to sawdust in my mouth, and I struggle to swallow it.

I am unable to find joy in what have previously been happy family activities, such as our regular days out to the park, or socialising with friends. I also have no desire to bake, something I've always enjoyed.

James has been burdened with the bulk of our joint responsibilities, the practical chores and running the household, all while I am rapidly falling apart.

I cannot shake the feeling that I have let my family down in a big way, which causes me to feel even more shame and self-loathing. As a result, I have started to shut my family out. I imagine that they will probably be better off without me. I envisage how easy it would be just to die and free myself from this emotional suffering.

I silently cry myself to sleep every night, praying for God to take away my pain. I must be the biggest failure the world has ever seen.

Tuesday, 31st March

James is having his car serviced today, so I've had to find the courage to venture out and pick him up from work.

On the drive home I am suddenly struck, from out of nowhere, with the now familiar sense of panic—that absolute feeling of dread and desperation. Terrifying emotions bubble up inside and began spewing forth, purging in a barrage of hateful words.

I psychotically scream from the driver's seat, "I CAN'T DO THIS ANYMORE! I WANT TO DIE! I'M GOING TO CRASH THIS CAR RIGHT NOW AND KILL MYSELF!"

James grabs the steering wheel and manages to get us safely to the side of the road. I am a mess. Crying, snotty and ranting on with a devastating tirade that simply makes no sense.

After my rage finally subsides, we both sit motionless in

the idling car. James turns in his seat to face me, gently grips my shoulders and looks lovingly into my eyes.

"I think we need to get you in to see someone," he says quietly, without judgement.

After calmly getting out of the car, he coaxes me into the passenger seat. I cry all the way home.

Welcome to rock bottom.

Thursday, 21st May

After my breakdown in the car, I was referred to a psychologist attached to my medical team.

I feel apprehensive about going to my first appointment, as I have often thought people who saw counsellors or psychologists were self-absorbed narcissists, suffering from a compelling need to talk about themselves and their imagined problems. However I'm so desperate for help, I'll need to put my preconceived ideas aside if I want to get on top of this.

The psychologist welcomes me as I take a seat opposite her in the gently-lit room. I am incredibly nervous, but her calm demeanour immediately puts me at ease. I sink into the cushioned armchair as she gently questions me about my recent experiences. I cry throughout the whole session.

It feels reassuring to finally have someone convince me that I'm not alone—that I'm not wrong or erroneous in my feelings and that the thoughts I have been having are perfectly normal and understandable. I don't have to hide it anymore. I don't have to be ashamed. I'm not a failure. I'm so relieved to recognise this.

The psychologist gives me concrete and practical advice on dealing with anxiety and how to manage those dark thoughts and re-establish healthy psychological functioning.

She helps me understand why this anxiety began by comparing a cancer experience with going to war: in both situations, you're just trying to survive. Returning to normal life after treatment is similar to a soldier returning home after combat, she says. With time to process every painful experience, the anxiety emerges as a delayed reaction to severe psychological shock. People may think you're lucky to have survived, but they have no idea what you *went* through to survive. She explains how any traumatic experience can have a devastating and lasting effect on a person's mental and emotional well-being.

As the session concludes, I realise having an experienced professional to talk through my issues with and understand what I'm going through is valuable beyond my expectations.

As I leave the clinic, I notice the deciduous trees lining the street where my car is parked. It is the end of autumn, and most of the trees have already shed their leaves, except for one tree, its branches full of lifeless, dry leaves.

A strong wind begins to blow through the branches, but the dead leaves still cling tight. Are the leaves hanging on to the tree? Or is the tree hanging on to the leaves that it no longer needs? Does the tree not realise that new leaves will appear in spring, fresh and vibrant? Am I clinging to a part of me that is no longer needed? What do I need to let go of that no longer serves me? Perhaps it's time to rid myself of the tendency to expect the worst and make room for better things to come into my life.

I find that my anxiety is worse in the mornings. In these early hours, before the rest of my family is awake, my mind is foggy and scattered. This is the time I am most vulnerable to that bitchy voice in my head taking over, telling me about all the bad stuff that could potentially happen. As I lay in bed, becoming more and more anxious, my stomach ties itself in knots until I literally give myself a stomach upset.

The psychologist had suggested that instead of lying in bed with my worries swirling around in my head, becoming more destructive the longer I lay there, I should get out of bed immediately upon waking, dress and head out for a quick ten-minute walk. The daylight and fresh air may help wake me up properly, she said, so I can better manage the dark thoughts before they get out of hand. I have never been a lover of rising early, especially not to exercise, but I decide to give it a go. I have nothing to lose.

Friday, 22nd May

Waking up at dawn, I immediately jump out of bed, hurriedly dress and step out into the misty morning air.

As I cross the street and head down the path towards the park, I marvel at the jewelled frost on the tips of long grass, which shimmer in the morning light. Ducks bob across the smooth, cool water of the pond, going about their business of preening themselves and foraging for food. The early morning joggers and walkers are all so friendly and eager to say a cheery "Hello!" as I pass.

This walk is probably the most magical stroll I have ever taken, and it completely changes my perspective on life. I've discovered so many things I never noticed before. After seeing my neighbourhood—and my world—in a whole new light, I realise now that I have been missing out on this for years!

In this simple act of stepping outside, I've discovered relief from being stuck in my head, ruminating with negative thoughts, and this change in mindset continues once I get home. Finally, I have a way to get a handle on those dysfunctional thoughts.

ANXIETY

Thursday, 23rd July

One of the things I still need to get a hold of is what I call 'medical anxiety'. I seem to have extreme reactions to anything medically related—such as seeing the doctor for a checkup—even if I'm not the patient being examined.

Simply being in a medical setting, like a doctor's waiting room, is enough to cause me to start hyperventilating. This makes it extremely difficult to perform my parental duties in taking my kids to the doctor or the dentist.

The traumatic experience of my initial diagnosis, coupled with being present in the doctor's surgery when Mum was given her grave prognosis, has left me with intense fear.

I have to undergo some pelvic and abdominal ultrasounds today, due to having prolonged pain in my stomach for the past few days. James, ever supportive, wanted to come with me, but I've decided that I need to try and face these fears on my own.

Sitting nervously in the waiting room, I breathe slowly and tell myself I will be okay. I concentrate on the little indoor plant next to my chair, attempting to consciously focus my awareness on the present moment, instead of skipping ahead to a frightening imagined future. I try to connect with the energy of the plant, and I begin to feel the anxiety drain out as I catch a glimpse of the profound importance of centring myself in the present moment and taking things one step at a time.

I have my scans done, pick up the results and step out of the clinic feeling a little bit stronger than when I had walked in. Every baby step I take towards becoming more independent and less fearful helps me to move in the right direction.

The reactive way I have been dealing with medical events has been the source of my anxiety, rather than the situation itself. With each and every moment, I have a choice of how to think about and react to circumstances.

Every time a negative thought begins to enter my head space, it's a new opportunity for me to start to think differently. I need to acknowledge each negative thought, then gently, ever so gently, persuade my brain to let go of that thought and replace it with a better one.

By taking it gradually, in small degrees, perhaps I will learn that it's *always* my choice how I respond to every situation. I don't need to have a knee-jerk reaction to every thought.

Even though I have never considered this possibility before, I now see the potential and capacity to develop greater control over my thinking.

Tuesday, 11th August

The upside to being so far down on the mental and emotional scale, I've discovered, is that there is no place to go but up.

It only takes a single moment of clarity for healing to begin. True healing began to occur for me when I sought professional help to give me the support I needed. By acknowledging the suffering that was there, I allowed myself to fully *feel* the pain and rage simmering below the surface, instead of denying the presence of these emotions.

Sitting with my feelings, observing them, and allowing them to wash over me was my path to freedom. The fearful part of my mind initially resisted. It tried to convince me that it was safer to deny these uncomfortable feelings.

Though it was frightening to face the wounds and scars of the emotional trauma I have been through, the moment I honoured these feelings, they began to dissipate. By peeling back the layers of denial, I was able to see that ignoring the pain and fear required a lot more effort than merely allowing it to be present.

Facing my deepest fears is now a daily practice that allows me to get a little stronger and more resilient each day. Letting my thoughts run away on a negative path was damaging my self-esteem, so I am slowly beginning to train myself to stop these thoughts before they spiral out of control.

When someone mentions the word 'cancer', I now say to myself, "cancel." It's amazing how this simple action has begun to take the fear out of that word for me.

When I start to feel sorry for myself or compare my suffering to others, I tell myself, "stop," and direct my thoughts more positively. In redirecting my thoughts away from negativity, I have found that positive thoughts begin to flourish. This takes practice but, with mindful attention to my thoughts, I'm getting better at it each day.

Slowly I am beginning to emerge from the darkness of my diagnosis. I think back to all the times in my life when I had created my own stress, because my negative thinking was out of control, and I did not have the ability to change.

Throughout this whole cancer experience, I have learned so many essential life skills—some that I didn't even know I needed, but which are crucial to having peace of mind and a healthy outlook on life.

One of the greatest skills I have learned from this whole experience, is the ability to control my thinking. This is something that I had never realised was possible before now. I always thought that thinking was something that *happened* to me. I now know, from observation, experience and practice, that *I* am the thinker, and *I* have complete control over choosing to pay attention to my thoughts, if they are beneficial to me, or to dismiss them if they don't serve me well.

ANXIETY

Adversity forces you to think outside the box. It compels you to evolve. It drives the expansion of the mind and pushes you to learn more, do more and *be* more.

Suffering and hardship have pushed me to what I felt was the brink of insanity, forcing me to learn how to focus my thinking and let go of negative thoughts.

Being able to take a step back and observe my thoughts at any given moment is powerful and life-changing. Like anything in life, it becomes easier and easier to do with practice. This doesn't mean that adverse circumstances won't ever arise, but now I won't allow them to affect my peace of mind.

"Not till we are lost, in other words, not till we have lost the world, do we begin to find ourselves, and realise where we are and the infinite extent of our relations."

— Henry David Thoreau

Body Image

Friday, 4th September

Today marks one year since Boob-Voyage. I still have days where I am in mourning for my breasts. Complicated emotions are muddying up my usually ordered brain. Just because other people can't see that I have had a mastectomy doesn't make it any less real for me.

I'm not sure how to describe the feeling of my breast implants. The way my brain is processing the sensation is skewed, as though it doesn't know how to relay the feeling to me. It's like I have the rims of two large plastic cups tightly pressed against my chest. It's very odd indeed.

My entire chest feels weird. All the skin on it is completely numb, like I've been injected with a local anaesthetic. Sometimes I have pins and needles, and it feels like it's itching, but I get no relief when I scratch. I wonder if my chest will feel like this forever?

I've been rubbing my scars with lotion in an attempt to make them less visible. Hopefully, by massaging the area around my new breasts, my brain will begin to process the sensation and become accustomed to them. Maybe then they won't feel so foreign.

I am keenly aware that a massive chunk of my body has been taken away from me. Is this how limb amputees feel?

Sometimes I wonder about what happened to my breasts. Where did the doctors put them after they removed them? What did they look like sitting apart from my body during surgery? How the hell do these doctors and nurses see this kind of stuff day in and day out? It's a gruesome thought to have, but I just can't help thinking about it.

I've stumbled across an article published on *The We Belong Project*,[3] a website which helps healthcare providers connect with their patients in an empathetic partnership. In a post, titled "An Open Letter to My Patient on the Day of Her Mastectomy," nurse practitioner Niki shares her thoughts. These exquisitely beautiful words, written by an extraordinary human being, acknowledge the humanness of medical professionals, and their vulnerability to the emotional challenges they face each day while caring deeply about the wellbeing of their patients.

...

Hello, Dear.

Today is the day. I am a member of the surgical team who will take care of you—the team that will remove your breast to treat the cancer that has tried to make a home in your body. We all have our role today, and the world would see yours to be the 'patient'. I see it as something more: a powerful gift to us. Because you remind us why we do what we do.

Today will feel sterile and scary. And I am sorry for that. I wish there were a better way. Today we will ask you to take all your clothes off and put in their place a gown. Women before you have worn it. Women after you will wear it. Be sure to ask for warm blankets, because we always have plenty. We will ask of you your blood type, your medical history, your allergies. We will ask you to lie down in a bed that's foreign to you. We will have to poke you so that we can start an IV.

You will meet many nurses, doctors, and hospital employees. We will write down important things for you to know. Your surgeon will see you soon. He will have to mark the breast we are having to remove today.

We will take you into the Operating Room—a room only few have seen. There will be bright lights, lots of metal, instruments that you've never seen, and we will be dressed in gowns, gloves, and masks. Over our masks, we hope you can see our eyes reassuring you as you go off to sleep.

Today is the day you will have to say goodbye to a part of your body, a part of yourself.

Your breast has felt the warmth of a lover's caress, has fed your child with life-sustaining milk and connection. You have many memories stored in your breast, stories none of us today know about. Somehow I wish I knew them.

And yet. Here we are. We must do our rituals. We must scrub our arms and hands with alcohol so that we can fight off infection before we start. We don our gowns, our gloves, our masks. We must drape your body in blue.

You are exposed. And unconscious. And it must be difficult to trust. I honour you, Dear One.

My job is to help your surgeon take away the cancer. I get a bird's eye view of the process. The surgery begins, and I feel your warm skin through my gloves. I wonder what stories you already have and the ones that are yet to come.

We carefully remove your breast. It never gets easy to see or to do. *You must know this.* It never feels natural, it never feels cavalier. It feels sacred to me. Every. Single. Time.

I look down and see your *pectoralis major*—the big muscle behind your breast. A source of strength. It is beautiful and shiny. Sometimes it contracts a little bit while we work. Sometimes the muscle is bright red and young. Sometimes the muscle is faded a little. But it is always strong. I like to gently touch it with my fingers. Because I feel your strength there.

We must send your breast away now. It officially leaves your body. I always feel an ache in my gut in that moment. There is no way for you to fully prepare for this day, Dear One.

I like to think that your body is already healing, as we close the incision we had to make.

Sewing your skin back together feels like I'm helping a little. But I know it's actually all *you* doing the work. Even as you sleep, Dear One.

We will put a bandage on your incision. We will wake you up. We will tell you everything went well. But the road is just beginning for you.

I saw you today.

You are beautiful.

You are strong.

Thank you for entrusting me and my colleagues with your most intimate moments. I am honoured to be a witness to this phase of your life.

Because now the healing begins. Now the grief is in full force. Now your breast is gone and in its place is a memory.

I watch you as you wake up. And I want to make it all go away. I can't. Today your body underwent a transformation. And today our team took care of your body. I hope we took care of your heart, too.

There is nothing we can say or do to make it go away. But please know that I care. *We care.* Behind our masks and gowns are heavy hearts and sometimes tears.

Yours are a gift today. Because you remind us of human resilience. You remind us of strength. You remind us of trust.

I saw you today.

You are beautiful.

You are strong.

I will not forget.

Niki, your Nurse Practitioner First Assistant on the Surgical Team.

This incredibly powerful piece of writing has had a massive impact on me. Clearly, the author is another guardian angel in human form, sent to share her thoughts with the world and guide those in need towards the healing of their bodies and their emotions. Her words have touched me deeply and have made me feel honoured and respected as both a person and a patient.

Tuesday, 8th September

I am still having trouble accepting how my body now looks. Even though I am grateful for the mastectomy having saved my life, I am shocked and discouraged every time I look in the mirror and see my changed form. It's as though I've lost my femininity and my identity as a woman.

Our bodies go through so many changes during our lifetime, but frequently we find it hard to accept and embrace these changes. I know I'm not the only woman in the world to have body image issues, as I've never met a woman who was completely happy with the way she looked. We think our boobs are too saggy, our thighs too wobbly, or our tummies too round.

This body-image distortion seems to start early in life. If

we have curly hair, we want straight hair. If we have straight hair, we want curly. We want to be slimmer, taller and have bigger boobs. We want to have clearer skin, longer eyelashes and fuller lips. We even want to halt the ageing process.

As we grow up, we come to focus on our physical image in relation to how we perceive it appears to others. We just can't seem to accept that we are all different—that we are all perfectly beautiful just the way we are. Of course not, we're women! We love to analyse, compare, nitpick and judge ourselves and our bodies to the *nth* degree.

Throughout my adult life, I mostly felt happy in my own skin. The shape or size of my body, as it went through its many changes during pregnancy and breastfeeding, but also as I have aged, never felt like a big issue. I always felt desirable and desired by my husband.

However, since my diagnosis, I have undergone a complete personality change. Gone is the happy, confident woman I once was. In her place is a scared, neurotic shadow—one who continually questions and compares herself with every other woman she sees.

Never before in my life have I felt the need to compete with or compare myself to other women, yet now I do this daily. When I go out, every woman I see appears to be flaunting herself, with her perky breasts and perfect body. I wonder if my husband notices these flawless women? Even though I try so hard to deny my feelings, I am jealous of women who still have real breasts and nipples. I feel so ugly and unattractive.

The anxiety caused by these groundless comparisons is getting out of control. My confidence and self-esteem are at an all-time low. I am plagued with unfounded fears about being unattractive because I've lost what I thought made me a woman—my breasts. In their place, I now bear disfiguring scars.

I continually wonder whether James is still attracted to me. Even though I look normal in clothing, due to having the breast reconstruction, whenever I look in the mirror at my naked self, all I see is a nipple-less 'Barbie' doll, with grotesque scars and short, boyish hair instead of my once long and glossy tresses. I harshly judge my appearance in the mirror: eunuch-like, sexless and unfeminine. I wonder how, if ever again, my husband could possibly be turned on by this unattractive sight.

Unexpectedly, I have begun to focus on other body issues that never concerned me before. I've become obsessed with watching my weight. I monitor everything I eat, mentally calculating the calories and how much exercise I will need to do afterwards.

How did my body image become so radically and severely distorted? Where did these deep-seated insecurities about my worth come from? Do I feel that I am not *enough?* That I am somehow deficient as a woman because I have no breasts, nipples or long hair anymore? These are all physical traits that, in the past, I thought were essential to my attractiveness and appeal as a woman.

At times it seems like there are two of me: the real 'me', who wants to be the positive and happy person I used to be, and another 'me', my ego, who is bitchy and demoralising, intent on destroying what's left of my self-esteem. When I look at myself in the mirror, it says to me, "You're not a *real* woman anymore." Seriously? This is insanity.

Saturday, 12th September

I carefully scrutinise James' facial expressions and body language, looking for subtle indications that he might find me hideous and ugly. I watch him like a hawk whenever he interacts with women, expecting to catch him flirting at every opportunity.

Whenever he leaves the house, even to go to work, I imagine him meeting someone else and comparing this beautiful, new woman to the hideous and repulsive person I have become. In this horrid scenario in my mind, things never end well for me.

I recognise that these vile and destructive thoughts are

self-sabotaging, but I am unable to control it. *Am I losing my mind?* How, after nearly twenty years of marriage, could I possibly think that my husband's love for me is dependent on the way my body looks? I don't for a minute regret my decision to have a mastectomy—I know, without a doubt, that it was the best decision for me—but I did not foresee the emotional spin that it would put me into.

I hesitantly find the courage to open up and talk to James about my insecurities, revealing to him the depth of my chaotic thoughts and my intense fear that he may be repulsed by my appearance.

Relief washes over as he reassures me that he still finds me exceedingly attractive, that he loves my body just the way it is and that I am as beautiful today as the day he married me. He affirms his love for the person I am on the inside and assures me that his feelings for me have not changed. He vows he will never leave me—no matter what. This moment of heartfelt compassion and reassurance, from the man I love, is instantly healing.

Wednesday, 16th September

I'm eager to understand how my body image and sexuality have become inexplicably crippled by my distorted mental state. Researching the effect that mastectomy and cancer can have on the mind, I discover an article on the Internet by Professor Jane Ussher, from the University of Western Sydney, who has extensively studied the psychological relationship between sexuality and cancer.

In her article, titled "Perceived causes and consequences of sexual changes after cancer for women and men: a mixed method study," Professor Ussher states:

> ...*many women participants attributed sexual changes after cancer to body image concerns, and to feeling unattractive as a consequence of sexual changes. This supports previous reports that cancer can serve as an 'invisible assault to femininity', associated with diminished gender identity, and feelings of lack of sexual attractiveness and sexual confidence. Socio-cultural constructions of idealised femininity normalise sexually attractive women as thin and young, with intact breasts signifying desirability. Whilst such 'emphasised femininity' is often unattainable, it is a core cultural ideal that shapes many women's experiences of embodiment. As the present study shows, these constructions impact on women's sexual practices and subjectivity post-cancer – leading many of the participants feeling that they are now noncompliant with femininity, because they are reportedly 'inadequate', 'fat', 'different', 'grotesque' and 'sexually unattractive'.*[4]

Reading through her study, I realise that I am not alone in how I feel about my body. Some of the participants stated they felt as though their body was hideous and repulsive. Others reported feelings of inadequacy and doubt about their sexual attractiveness, self-esteem and body image after having gone through the experience of cancer, especially cancers which affected sexual or reproductive body areas. This lack of physical and sexual self-esteem seems to be a common theme for many post-cancer patients.

I am slowly beginning to appreciate that it all comes down to completely accepting my new—and now healthy—body. It may look different, but it is not diminished. I am not *less* than I was before.

I would never think anything less of a person if they were missing an arm, a leg or any other body part for that matter. So why should I think less of myself? I am still a whole person. Unique and irreplaceable.

Saturday, 17th October

I've downloaded a meditation app to my phone, and I've been learning to meditate to help process the feelings I am having. This way of exploring my emotions has lead me to realise that I have to move forward with complete acceptance to heal my body-image issues.

It's been difficult to face these raw emotions, but it has also been extraordinarily enlightening and cathartic. I am learning to love myself and find my own peace.

I won't gain solace from looking to my husband or to any other person. I have to look inward, into the depths of my soul and realise that I have everything I need already inside. I know I have the strength, the acceptance and the self-esteem, I just have to let it rise to the surface and anchor it there! I must stop letting myself down.

I'm gradually starting to understand how my body image had become distorted, due to my lack of acceptance of the changes to my body. I should be proud of the fact that my scars show my strength and my courage.

I've been through some tough times that would have ruined many people, but I have emerged like a phoenix from the ashes—reborn, regenerated, renewed and stronger than ever. I am confident and eager to get on with my life. I am not limited or lacking. I am enough. I am not in competition with anyone else. I do not need to try to be better than anyone else.

I am still whole.

I am still real.

I am still 'me'.

I didn't choose to get cancer, but I did choose to have the mastectomy. Maybe if I didn't, I would have died. I choose life!

When I was gowned up ready to go into the operating theatre before my surgery, my surgeon mentioned the mole on my breast which he said would be removed along with my breasts. He then pointed to a big, brown, raised mole on my stomach and asked, "Do you want me to take that off as well?"

Having thought about it for a minute, I replied, "No." I explained that I'd had that mole forever. It's part of my *imperfect* perfection, what makes me, well, 'me'.

The surgeon smiled. I could only guess what he was thinking, but I hope it was, "You're right. Perfect is boring."

"A diamond with a flaw is worth more than a pebble without imperfections."

— Chinese proverb

Nipples

Monday, 19th October

There's a funny thing about nipples: like many things in life, you take them for granted. Until you don't have them anymore.

When I had the mastectomy, I was so relieved to be getting the cancer out of my body, I didn't give much thought to the long-term consequences, especially what life would be like without having nipples.

It sucks!

For such a seemingly insignificant part of the body—I mean it's not obvious like losing an arm or a leg—adapting to life without them has had substantial psychological implications. I could not be more acutely aware of their absence.

It is bizarre to look at my naked self in the mirror and see two nipple-less mounds on my chest. I look exactly like a Barbie doll, give or take a few kilos—and when I was going through chemotherapy I had no pubic hair like Barbie either!

The loss of my nipples has profoundly affected me, even more than the loss of my breasts. My sense of body image and self-image has dramatically changed, and my self-esteem has vastly diminished. I don't feel *feminine* anymore, and every time I see myself in the mirror, it's a stark reminder of all the trauma I've been through.

I avoid facing the painful reality by refusing to have my chest uncovered in front of James. I undress in the dark and spend little time bathing, quickly covering myself as I step out of the shower. My sex drive has diminished, and I feel unnatural and unattractive.

On the bright side, at least I don't have to worry about stiff nipples on cold days. And my chances of having a *nipple-gate* incident while wearing a bikini on the beach are non-existent. It's also perfectly legal to go topless when you have no nipples. I could walk down the main street of town topless, and the police couldn't charge me with public indecency. Who knew?

When I spoke to my surgeon on the subject of nipples, he said that older women who have had mastectomies don't seem to have an issue with being nipple-less. The over-fifties are least likely to opt for breast reconstruction after their mastectomy and, he said, it's mainly younger women who are concerned about their appearance post-surgery.

I wonder if this is related to libido and sexuality? Or is it purely a psychological issue for younger women? Could it be that older women are more likely to have a life partner who bears a few battle scars of their own? Younger women, who may still be searching for a partner, may feel that breasts and nipples are necessary to enhance their self-esteem.

No matter what age, I'm sure I will always be concerned about my appearance. I only need look at my bulging wardrobe or the amount of money I've spent on hairdressing and beauty treatments to see that.

Getting back to the two little issues at hand, the options for women in my situation to regain any normal appearance post-mastectomy, with regards to their nipples, is limited.

Information on nipple options has been difficult to find, but I think it is something that should be offered to all women facing mastectomy. It's enough that we've had to go through cancer. Perhaps doctors, surgeons and oncologists could initiate more conversations with patients about their needs post-mastectomy?

I've researched artists who specialise in three-dimensional tattoo art and can mimic the appearance of a nipple.

While the tattoos look incredibly realistic, the nipple is just a picture—a one-dimensional tattooed image with no texture or nipple-like protrusion.

Plastic surgeons can perform surgery to recreate a false nipple, and this can be enhanced by tattooing after the surgery has healed. I have read mixed reviews about this kind of procedure, and I am yet to meet any women who have had it done. From what I've discovered, the re-created nipple can flatten out over time. The tattoos, although effective at first, will fade over time like regular tattoos.

I came across a company in the United States that sells temporary 'nipple' tattoos. They were reasonably priced, so I ordered some online and was thrilled when they arrived.

Trying to apply two temporary tattoos to your chest, at precisely the same height as each other, is much harder than it sounds. I had a few lopsided mishaps before I managed to align them, but I was excited to see my new 'nipples'.

From a distance, they did look extremely realistic. However, I had to be careful not to wash too vigorously in the shower so they wouldn't wear off, and I quickly grew tired of having to reapply them.

After continuing my research, I discover another company, also in the United States, Pink Perfect[5], who make realistic 3D nipple prosthetics.

Designed by an artist who is a breast cancer survivor herself, the prosthetics are handmade from high-quality silicone, and have a similar look and feel to real nipples.

There are a variety of natural-looking colours to choose from, as well as three different nipple protrusions: 'modest', 'natural' or 'bold'. I immediately order the bold protrusion—now is not the time to be modest.

Friday, 6th November

It's not every day you receive a pair of nipples in the post. My prosthetics have arrived, and I am excited to try them out.

After attaching them to my chest with the supplied waterproof adhesive, I step back from the mirror. They are very realistic looking, and the boost to my sense of self-esteem, from having these two little silicone discs glued to my body, is immediate. They cover up some of the scars, and from a distance, if I squint, it looks like I have ordinary breasts and nipples. Finally, I can look at myself and feel *normal*.

I have started to wonder about the possibility of 3D-printed nipples. Hey, if scientists can 3D-print ears and other body parts, why not nipples?

A company named TeVido BioDevices[6] is developing propriety, patent-pending, bio-printing technology named Cellatier,™ and when combined with a woman's own living cells, will build a custom nipple-areola complex (NAC) graft.

TeVido's website goes on to say:

> *Studies highlight that patients with loss of the nipple and areola continue to experience psychological distress even long after breast mound reconstruction has taken place and recreation of the nipple-areola complex has a high correlation with overall patient satisfaction and acceptance of body image.*[7]

Although science is still a while away from 3D-bio-printed nipples becoming a reality, I have no doubt it will happen in my lifetime. I've asked my surgeon to get in contact with the company to put me on the list for clinical trials. Who knows, maybe I can help to enhance and improve the lives of many more women in the future.

Despite the unforeseen issues that have cropped up, I know, all in all, I have had a fantastic outcome from my surgery and cancer treatment. I am trying to liken my nipple-less state with someone who is bald or doesn't have teeth. I remember my beloved grandparents having dentures. They slept every night with their teeth in a glass of water next to their beds. They simply put their dentures back in every morning upon waking. No one ever looked at them and said, "You're not a real person because you don't have teeth!" What about balding men, who embrace their baldness by shaving their heads? They carry off their new look and somehow seem really *bad-ass.* No one thinks any less of them.

    I can either refuse to accept the changes to my body or work with the changes. The solution lies in my perspective. I remind myself to dig deeper and lean on the lessons I have learned so far in my journey. When I look in the mirror, I try to see myself as beautiful, perfect and healthy. I am grateful for the strength and resilience of my body, and I cherish it, flaws and all.

*"To be deeply loved by someone gives you strength,
but to love someone deeply gives you courage."*

— Esther Huertas

Marriage

Wednesday, 18th November

When you've been with someone for a long time, it's easy to become lazy and forget to tell or show your partner how much you love them. We may assume they know it, so we just stop expressing how we feel. It's not that we don't love them deeply, we do, it's just that life gets in the way. The pressures of raising a family, working and running a household can be overwhelming, and love sometimes gets put on the back-burner.

Before my diagnosis, James and I had reached that point in our marriage, as many couples do I suppose, where all we were doing was giving ourselves away. We had dedicated our lives to raising our children, working to pay off our mortgage and running around after the family in a myriad of ways, neglecting ourselves in the process and leaving our marriage depleted. We were not taking time for *us* and our relationship, and I think we were both feeling a bit empty and unfulfilled.

The cancer diagnosis shocked us into action. Amidst this life-altering experience, and facing the threat of death and the loss of everything we had built together, we realised how complacent we had become about the things that *really* mattered. We were jolted into awareness of how precious our marriage was and how much we stood to lose if we failed to care for it.

Our marriage is still profoundly tested by this cancer experience every day, but we have both made the commitment to try and make each day as special as possible. We are working hard to regain, strengthen and maintain our deep bond and connection. It's a gradual process, a bit like falling in love all over again, recommitting to each other with the intention to make our marriage the best it can be—rock solid and able to withstand any storm.

If we hadn't had this huge wake-up call, I'm not sure we would be in the positive place we are now. Through adversity came an opportunity for us to re-think our relationship and the flow-on effects to our family.

I recognise now that communication is *the* most important aspect of any relationship. Any misunderstanding, grievance or hurt can be instantly transformed and healed by a single moment of honest, *from-the-heart* communication.

Being physically intimate with James has been part of developing a deeper connection with one another. In order to 'bring sexy back' to our marriage, I took some small steps to improve my body image and self-esteem. Each day I found something positive and uplifting to tell myself about my body, such as, "My body is strong and energetic," or "My body is healthy and resilient."

I bought some racy new lingerie to spice things up. Although functionality has always been the *order of the day* for me—sensible cotton underwear and industrial strength, foundation-enhancing bras—I discovered that wearing underwear made from beautiful fabrics actually made me feel more sensual.

Wearing sexy lingerie has also enhanced our love life, as the visual focus is taken off my chest and I am able to feel more relaxed and confident.

James and I make an effort to be intimate on a more conscious level, and from this deeper mental, emotional and spiritual connection, I have become more confident in all areas of my self-esteem.

All marriages experience good times and bad. The cancer diagnosis had the potential to destroy our marriage, but I now look upon it as a blessing that brought us closer together.

I think back to our wedding day when we stood together in front of our family and friends at the church and made that vow to stick by each other 'in sickness and in health'. We could never have anticipated this cancer diagnosis, but in promising to each other that we would not leave when things got rough, we found strength in the dark times. We've been able to depend on each other when the going got tough. We have recommitted to each other and our family, and it has had so many positive effects on our relationship, making all that hard work worthwhile.

The Roman poet, Virgil, wrote: "Love conquers all things; let us too surrender to love." With love, all obstacles can be overcome, all mountains become molehills. With love, anything is possible.

MARRIAGE

*"There is nothing either good or bad,
but thinking makes it so."*

— William Shakespeare, *Hamlet,* (2.2.249)

Menopause

Monday, 8th February

The chemotherapy has caused one significant side effect—menopause. I'm still trying to make up my mind whether to view this from a positive or a negative perspective.

After panicking at the sight of the mid-cycle bleeding, right before my mastectomy, I was mystified to discover that I stopped menstruating after my surgery, and I began having severe hot flushes, day and night. After a series of blood tests, my doctor bluntly announced that I was now completely menopausal.

I can't believe I have reached my forties and know very little about menopause. I wish I had discussed this topic with

Mum while she was still alive. I know the basics, having heard various things here and there, but I have no first-hand knowledge about the emotional side of menopause or how it would affect me. I guess I will just have to *feel* my way through this.

The hot flushes, or 'hot flashes' as some people call them, are the most irritating symptom. Never in my life have I had such an unsettling sensation in my body. It feels like I'm suddenly heating up from my toes to the top of my head, like a dreadfully hot furnace is burning inside me.

When I feel the heat overtake my senses, I must immediately take off any jumper, jacket or whatever clothing I am wearing, even if I'm driving my car, or something equally as precarious.

Many times I've exclaimed to James, "Feel me! I'm boiling!" And he rolls his eyes and replies that my skin seems cool to him, even though I feel like I've heated up to a thousand degrees in an instant. A few moments later it subsides and, more often than not, I start to feel cold, shivering with goosebumps.

This process is annoying enough during the day, but it is when I am trying to sleep that it really bothers me. Every forty minutes or so I wake up from what feels like a sudden rush of adrenaline, followed by a surge of heat, causing me to throw the blankets off dramatically. The sensation of heat dissipates, and then I begin to feel freezing cold. This doesn't make for a very restful night's sleep, for me or for James! I can't remember the last time I had a full, undisturbed sleep. I seriously could look after a new baby again!

One exasperating symptom—although I'm not sure if it's from menopause or chemotherapy—is memory loss. When I speak, I often forget words mid-sentence or get mixed up with what I want to say. It's frustrating and makes me feel terribly dense at times.

Another disturbing development has been weight gain. After having lost so much weight early on during my diagnosis, now I seemingly gain weight just by looking at food. It's discouraging to see my body expand so quickly. None of my clothes fit properly anymore, and that makes me feel worse.

My oncologist told me that weight gain can also be a side-effect of the estrogen-blocking medication that I am taking. He said most women on this medication gain around a kilogram a year. Well, I think I have gained ten years' worth already! I'm going to have to be extremely vigilant with my eating habits and exercise regularly if I want to remain on the lighter end of the scale. Now, there's an additional reason for getting my morning walk in each day.

Every time I turn around there seems to be a new challenge to deal with. Even though it's frustrating, I've decided there's nothing I can do but accept the situation and get on with my life.

But there are some positive effects too. After menstruating more or less monthly since age thirteen, except for during my pregnancies, not having to deal with pads and tampons, and all the hassle associated with periods, is liberating.

I've also noticed a complete change in my disposition. I used to have a clear and specific time, premenstrually, where I was moody, emotional and generally a pain to live with. Apart from ongoing anxiety, my mood is becoming more stable now I'm going through menopause, and I feel more in control of my emotions in general.

Life has a habit of changing quickly, and it seems that my whole world changed overnight. However, I choose to embrace this experience as a 'rite of passage', picturing the changes peeling away like layers of old paint, allowing a more resilient version of me to emerge.

Navigating my way through this new season of life is going to take some getting used to, but I will rise to every new challenge, one hot flush at a time.

MENOPAUSE

*"The windows of my soul I throw
Wide open to the sun."*

— John Greenleaf Whittier, *My Psalm*

Balance

Sunday, 28th February

In moving away from an anxious state of mind to a healthy and peaceful state of mind, I have tried many different practices and activities. Some of them became extremely useful in helping me to live my life in an entirely different way, and I've since embraced these practices into my daily life.

Before my cancer experience, I had so many ideas in my head about things I wanted to do and achieve, always telling myself, "I'll get around to trying that one day," but of course 'one day' was always in the distant future. I *put off* living my life to the fullest, believing that my needs were not important and living like many women do, always looking after everyone else first. By denying my innermost desires, I was chipping away at my soul and fading like a quilt in the summer sun.

Having cancer caused me to realise I had been missing the point of life because I assumed there would always be more time to do the things I wanted to do. I am now intensely aware of how important it is to make every moment count.

As life began to return to 'normal' after my treatment finished, I tried not to get bogged down in the busy-ness of life again. I found that once I began to follow my gut instincts and find my 'flow', new ways to live started to emerge.

When I invest in myself, even in a small way, everybody wins. By filling any void in my life with something that lifts me up to a higher level, I rejuvenate my soul. I am then able to give *more* to those I love.

Living this way has opened up new realms for me, and I have discovered many new interests, hobbies and activities. Not everything suited me, but each new activity or undertaking then led me onto something else, and I began to surrender to the natural flow of life. By getting out of my comfort zone, my innate dynamism, vitality and zest for life returned.

I read every book I could find about mindfulness, in the hope that incorporating mindful practices might help bring balance into my life. I wrote down and reflected on my desires at that moment, my deepest hopes and wishes of what

I really wanted out of life:

To be mentally strong and confident.
To love my life and experience joy every day.
To maintain a sense of peace, no matter what life throws at me.
To fully realise that I am 'enough' and be content with that.

After pondering my list, I began to think about how I could achieve my heart's desires. I attended a self-help seminar, where I was taught about the benefits of meditation. I had never tried it before my diagnosis—I always thought meditation was the domain of hippies and unconventional drop-outs. However, I decided I had nothing to lose. Of course, having children in the house means privacy is in rare supply, but I took a brief moment, while the boys were busy playing, to sit and listen to a guided meditation, trying not to get too caught up worrying about whether or not I was doing it 'right'.

I closed my eyes and focused on my breathing, slowly drawing air in through my nose, holding for a moment, then breathing out through my mouth, while imagining myself letting go of any emotions or negative thoughts I had been holding onto. When my mind began to wander, I felt frustrated that I couldn't stop thinking about my day-to-day life, the grocery list, how many chores I still had to do, what someone had said to me yesterday or how I should have responded. I tried not to judge these thoughts and, instead, I brought my attention back to my breathing.

Despite laughing at me at first and saying how silly Mummy looked, my children soon learned that this was my quiet time and they took it upon themselves to leave me undisturbed.

Far from merely being a way to relax, meditation has become a daily practice I use to connect with my inner self for guidance and to create positive focus. Through regular meditation, I have found peace and acceptance of all the circumstances of my life.

In the past, I would look too far into the future and wonder: *How could I possibly...?* I would then become overwhelmed and afraid of failure, eventually abandoning my goal.

Meditation has become a valuable tool for centring my mind in the 'now' moment of my life. It helps me to realise how important *right now* is, allowing me to stay calm within the 'eye of the storm' of my daily life. It has enabled me to release the negative thought patterns and beliefs which had built up due to the traumas I have experienced.

I meditate every day. No exceptions. I don't need to do it for long, ten minutes is ideal. It's helpful to meditate in the afternoon when I am feeling low after a busy day, or before a party or social gathering where I will be interacting with a lot of people. I find that when I communicate with others after meditating, I am more relaxed and serene.

When I was first diagnosed with cancer, I struggled to get going at the start of the day and complete my everyday tasks. I battled to process the overwhelming emotions that were weighing me down and I had trouble making even the simplest decisions. I was paralysed with fear and almost completely numb most of the time—it felt like I was wading through wet cement.

In the depths of my despair, I sometimes turned to social media, looking for distraction and reassurance to ease my mind. It often seemed that the right words of wisdom would pop up when I needed them most. I began copying down these inspirational quotes and sticking them up on the walls of my kitchen, where I could see them first thing every morning. I only liked to look at happy, uplifting words of pure, positive love.

I'm a firm believer that the right words and images will show up in life when I need them, that it's the Universe working in alignment with my highest good. I have found that sometimes, just reading something positive can dramatically improve my mood and outlook on life.

I was never a huge fan of drinking plain water, but during

chemotherapy, I needed to continually hydrate to flush the medication through my system. I cut out soft drinks and other caffeinated beverages. Plain water became my drink of choice, and I found I had fewer headaches, my constipation was alleviated, and many other areas of my health improved.

When it comes to my diet, I believe that everything in moderation is the key to living a healthy and enjoyable life. I don't restrict what I eat, but I try to include fresh fruit and plenty of vegetables with every meal. Getting cancer was a real wake up call for me to modify my diet and introduce more healthful foods. I am now mindful of what I put on my plate, and I try and make every bite count so that it will have a positive effect on my health.

Exercise has also had a significant impact on my overall health. I try to do something active every single day. There are so many free activities available, I don't need a gym membership or exercise equipment. I started walking, discovering I had a perfectly good footpath right outside my house—no need to buy an expensive treadmill.

Walking has improved my mental state as well as my physical body. The hardest part about exercise is starting. At first, I found it difficult as I was quite unfit but, within a relatively short period, my fitness began to improve, and each walk around the block got easier. Instead of taking my car, I now walk to work or to the shops. Once a week

I walk with my friend, Deb. We call our time together our 'hour of power'. I honestly could not imagine life without my daily walk.

My sleep patterns changed dramatically following my diagnosis. With so many worries on my mind, I often had trouble falling asleep. My frantic brain couldn't relax or switch off. Early menopause nearly sent me insane with hot flushes waking me up throughout the night, leaving me tired all day long. It's no wonder my body was crying out for a break. Now, whenever I notice I'm slowing down and feeling tired, I take time to refresh myself with a rest, even if it means I have to sleep during the day. I like to tell people that I imitate my cat—I nap whenever I can.

I have ramped up my efforts to make my personal relationships with family and friends my number one priority. I've made the choice to switch off the television, turn off my phone or computer and talk to my loved ones. Without these rewarding and fulfilling relationships, my life would lack meaning.

Growing up, I learned a lot from watching how my mother conducted herself. She was never too busy to lend a hand to a friend in need, or offer a shoulder to cry on when times were tough.

The front door of our home was like a revolving door. Arriving home from school, I never knew who was going to be sitting at our kitchen table, receiving some much-needed advice and counselling from Mum. Her wisdom was simple and easy to understand—everyone wanted to be near her.

Mum lived an incredible life because she genuinely cared about others. Family mattered above all else and she closely monitored the nurturing she gave her relationships with us. Of course, we had our share of family dramas—I don't know of any family that doesn't—but our difficulties were always resolved with love and deep care, never from a selfish perspective.

Mum left no loose ends. Nothing was left unsaid, good or bad, and every issue was straightened out before it became overwhelming. I know, without a doubt, that I was deeply loved and cherished. Now, while navigating motherhood with my own boys, I realise how lucky I was to have had such an incredible role model to look up to and emulate.

Seeking emotional support from family members and trusted friends has been paramount to my recovery. Everyone needs someone to talk things through with when going through a rough time. The encouraging words from those who love me kept me on an even keel when I was feeling desperate and my emotions were out-of-control.

What we say and do flows out to others, connecting us all, though we do not always consciously realise this. By helping each other through challenging times, we grow stronger and become more deeply fulfilled. Giving and receiving love is what makes life truly fulfilling and satisfying.

Many people have come forward, both friends and strangers alike, and shown such kindness and compassion, in the form of cooking meals, helping to look after my children or visiting to cheer me up. I am forever grateful to these kind souls who have done so much for me.

I've decided to 'pay it forward' to others who have also found themselves in difficult circumstances by making a commitment to myself to help others out, even if it is only a prayer or a kind word that I can offer. Focusing on other people's needs rather than my own helps me just as much as it does them, as it aids me in becoming less preoccupied with my own worries.

I like to cook, so I always bring a homemade treat when I visit someone, and I help by delivering meals to friends who are facing illness or other life challenges.

Every so often my family and I will challenge ourselves to undertake random acts of kindness, such as paying for the person behind us in line to get a coffee, helping someone carry their groceries when they are struggling, or delivering bottles of cold water and morning tea to the road workers near our house.

Little gestures can mean a lot to those in need. I am convinced that a tiny ripple of kindness can create a tidal wave of happiness. Paying it forward makes my life full, complete and satisfying.

I love this line from a poem by Sufi poet Hafiz:

Even after all this time, the sun never says to the earth,
"You owe me." Look what happens with a love like that,
it lights the whole sky.

Life is short. I want to have fun, enjoy it and not waste a single moment. The shock of my cancer diagnosis caused me to stop and take stock of my life. One of the big questions I began to ask myself was: *Why am I here?*

I came across a quote that said, "Are you really living life, or are you just paying bills until you die?" It's easy to get caught up in the *ordinary-ness* of life. But I genuinely believe that I am here to experience great joy. I keep this in the forefront of my mind to help me remember to inject light-heartedness into my life.

I think it's important to have something good to look forward to, so I plan joyful events and schedule in 'fun' time whenever I can.

I bought a red checkered tablecloth and initiated a tradition of Sunday family picnics. Every time I pack our picnic basket, the tablecloth is the first thing to go in. Our picnics are not elaborate, we throw a few sandwiches and bottles of water into the basket and head off to the nearest park to bask in the sunshine and the love of our family. This humble checkered tablecloth has come to symbolise our sacred family time. It brings a smile to my face whenever I see it.

Our annual family reunion is a day the whole family relishes. Everyone brings a plate of food, and we have sack races, ball games and our now-famous—and hilariously funny—watermelon-eating competition, It's a day of fun and connection that I look forward to all year.

One of Mum's favourite words was 'salubrious', meaning health-giving, and she used that word all the time to describe something awesome. In a nod to her influence, I have initiated something I've named 'salubrious schemes'—activities and pursuits that are health-giving and make me sparkle.

In no particular order these are some of the things that light me up: snorkelling, eating gelato, gazing at a sunset, having a water-balloon fight with my kids, eating fish and chips on the beach, talking to my friends, kayaking, scrapbooking, kissing my husband, watching fireworks, and dancing around the house to my awesome eighties music playlist. I always make sure I have plenty of salubrious schemes in my life, as they can be some of the sweetest moments.

I open my mind to new possibilities when they arise. I call this 'reading the signs', and I endeavour to follow their path. If something comes into my awareness and it interests me, instead of putting it into the 'too hard' basket and telling myself I don't have enough time, money, skills, or knowledge, I pursue it.

I've met and talked with fascinating people. I have read compelling books on topics that I had never thought would interest me before. I've tried new forms of exercise, meditation, yoga, self-help seminars, energy healing, you name it! I even swam naked in a charity ocean swim, *The Sydney Skinny,* to raise money for brain cancer.

I now feel as though life is offering me a sumptuous buffet of wonderful choices. Life truly is a gift.

BALANCE

"Your wings already exist, all you have to do is fly."

— Unknown

Identity

Thursday, 4th August

I'm beginning to dislike it when people refer to me as a 'breast cancer survivor'. I find it irritating but, at the same time, a little curious. At what point did I metamorphose from being a breast cancer *patient* to a breast cancer *survivor?*

While searching online for answers, I discovered this interpretation:

> *The transition from patient to survivor is different for everyone. Some see themselves as a survivor from when they become free from signs of cancer. Others see themselves as a survivor when active treatment stops. For many people,*

'survivor' is a strong and positive term. However, others feel it implies that they will struggle to cope with cancer in the future. Some people do not like being labelled at all and may prefer to put their cancer experience in the past. You may find it difficult to relate to the title of 'survivor' because you believe your treatment was relatively simple. Instead, you may refer to yourself as someone who has had cancer or is living with cancer.[8]

The mainstream media references that filter into the human psyche would have us believe that the way to approach adversity is with force. Whether it's the 'fight against cancer' or the 'war on drugs', *everything* potentially becomes a battle to be fought, lest we become the victim.

Making the disease or dysfunction the enemy provides something tangible to combat, and hating it is the method used to make it go away. A real problem begins, however, when these thoughts of hating and fighting start to define our very existence. When I've tried to fight or force a situation, it actually grew stronger in my mind, and I became consumed by the very thing that I was hating, forcing, or fighting. Force creates counter-force.

When newsreaders report the deaths of well-known celebrities or famous actors, they never simply announce the person has died, they almost always say, "They lost their

IDENTITY

brave battle against cancer." Why should this small portion of their life—their illness and how they died—become such a big focus, worthy of reporting in ghoulish detail? It seems terribly unfair to diminish a human life in this way.

The focus on cancer patients to be courageous and brave seems to indicate that those who do not feel courageous or brave—I certainly didn't—are failures if an air of bravado cannot be maintained during their illness.

By referring to me as a survivor, are people somehow indicating I've won the fight? Was there a fight in the first place? Or was it just an experience that, happily for me, didn't claim my life? Saying I survived breast cancer seems to be the same as saying I survived childbirth. Yes, both were dangerous and potentially life-threatening situations, but they were *experiences*. I experienced childbirth. I experienced cancer. I learned many valuable lessons from both, and they have become part of the tapestry of my life story. But they are not *the* story of my life.

Problems can occur if we define our identity by our fight. Some of the people I've spoken to who have been through cancer have, to varying degrees, made cancer their *entire* life story. They distinguish themselves as being a 'cancer patient', even though they are now healthy, and they have incorporated their cancer experience into their identity, weaving the story of their experience into every conversation.

I am all too conscious of the reasons people do this. I did it myself at first, and I became consumed by what I now call the 'poor me syndrome'. I used the sad tale of what I had been through in order to avoid situations, such as having to socialise, or to enhance my ability to control others ("Oh yes! Please do my ironing for me. I haven't been feeling well.") Without realising, I had become hooked on the drama of it. By manipulating people to do things out of pity and feel sorry for me, I could play the 'victim' and make them feel guilty about their own good health or fortune.

By maintaining this cancer patient identity, I was damaging my psyche in so many ways, and sabotaging my ability to move on with my life, for fear that I would no longer receive the attention I had become addicted to. I later realised this was a harmful and self-destructive way to operate as a human being.

There's nothing wrong with telling my story—storytelling is how information is passed on through the ages and handed down through the generations. In sharing what I have been through, I can convey valuable lessons. However, I have to remember that it is now just a story. By reliving the negative aspects of the past in my mind, I make it my reality, even though the experience itself no longer exists, except in my thoughts. It's not happening right *now*. It did happen, but it's over. I don't want to continue carrying these negative thoughts with me forever, nor do I want to colour every precious, present moment by looking through the fractured lens of the past.

When the sad details of a cancer experience become the narrative, it may create a huge imbalance that can only have a detrimental effect on a person's identity. Instead, I simply need to observe these previous events, take heed of the lessons they presented and then move on to enjoying my now healthy, present life. By viewing my circumstances from a more positive, balanced perspective, my story can then have a healing and transformational purpose.

I've discovered a blog[9] by an inspirational woman, Aniela McGuinness, who had a very similar experience to my own. I find it comforting to read she also has an aversion to being referred to as a 'survivor'. She prefers the term 'cancer graduate'. I love that. How fitting! Along with co-founder Nora McMahon, Aniela has begun a new project, Cancer Grad®, which offers support to readers and the opportunity to redefine their cancer experience from a 'war' to an 'education'.[10]

I have now begun to appreciate that having cancer has brought me so much more than it took away. It has given me a new perspective, forcing me to re-evaluate what is truly important. I am now conscious of the parts of my life that no longer fit, and this has compelled me to recalibrate all areas of my life—relationships, work, hobbies and passions—modifying and revising them until they feel balanced.

I have faced some of my worst fears, gained wisdom from working through them, and emerged stronger than ever before. Like a baptism of fire, this cancer experience has brought into the light all the dark facets of my life. I don't have time for unimportant, trivial aspects anymore—gossip, silly fights, resentment, or arguing over whose turn it is to take out the garbage—these things don't matter.

I want to live the fullest life possible. The realisation that my time on Earth is limited—just a drop in the ocean in the whole scheme of things—has made me stop and take inventory of my life. I no longer live life on the surface—I dive right in. I say *yes* to life. I didn't survive cancer just to watch more television.

I've made the decision to experience joy in every moment that I can. I no longer hold back in life. I don't wait to tell people how much they mean to me. I express my feelings to others because I now realise how important it is to make sure those around me know, without a doubt, how much I truly love and cherish them.

The landscape of my existence has changed dramatically over the past year and a half. I have reduced the pace of my life to an enjoyable tempo, and I take time for myself when I need to, instead of rushing around trying to satisfy the needs of others and neglecting my soul's callings. By making space for myself, I create room to breathe.

I now choose to live life deliberate in my actions. I enjoy time in my garden, basking in the sun with my cat. I take pleasure in sitting side-by-side with my husband while we drink our morning coffee and talk about everything and nothing. I love taking my boys camping and enjoying quality time together in nature.

My *being* is now filled with more purpose and meaning than I ever thought possible. I wake up every morning, eager to explore another magical day on this planet. I am grateful for every blessing I have been given and this opportunity to *really* begin living.

Having cancer has made me treasure every single moment, and embrace it all for what it really is: this experience of life.

Through suffering, I've learned to fully accept my body, scars and all. I can now embrace myself for who I truly am, and appreciate the fact that I am a unique individual with something important to offer the world.

In losing my breasts, I found myself.

*In memory of my mother,
Denise Ann Fleming.*

References

Diagnosis

1. en.wikipedia.org. (2019). *Kübler-Ross model.* [online] Available at: https://en.wikipedia.org/wiki/Kubler-Ross_model [Accessed 20 Aug. 2014].

Chemotherapy

2. https://www.lgfb.org.au

Body Image

3. Flemmer, N. (2013). *An Open Letter to My Patient on the Day of Her Mastectomy.* [online] The We Belong Project. Available at: https://www.thewebelongproject.com/blog/open-letter-mastectomy-patient [Accessed 4 Sep. 2015].

4. Ussher. J. M., Perz, J., & Gilbert, E. (2015), Perceived causes and consequences of sexual changes after cancer for women and men: a mixed method study. *BMC Cancer,* 15(268), 2-15. doi:10.1186/s12885-015-1243-8.

Nipples

5. Pink Perfect. (2015). *Adhesive Nipple Prosthesis | Custom Made Adhesive Nipples | Pink Perfect*. [online] Available at: https://www.pink-perfect.com [Accessed 19 Oct. 2015].

6. TeVido BioDevices. (2015). *TeVido BioDevices – Reconstructing Hope*. [online] Available at: http://www.tevidobiodevices.com [Accessed 6 Nov. 2015].

7. Evans, K., Rasko, Y., Lenert, J. and Olding, M. (2005). The Use of Calcium Hydroxylapatite for Nipple Projection After Failed Nipple-Areolar Reconstruction. *Annals of Plastic Surgery,* 55(1), pp.25-29.

Identity

8. cancervic.org.au. (2016). *Living well after cancer – Cancer Council Victoria*. [online] Available at: https://www.cancervic.org.au/living-with-cancer/life-after-treatment/living-well-after-cancer [Accessed 4 Aug. 2016].

9. https://www.mybreastchoiceshow.com

10. https://www.cancergrad.org

www.ingramcontent.com/pod-product-compliance
Lightning Source LLC
Chambersburg PA
CBHW051944290426
44110CB00015B/2109